THE KETO KIDS

COOKBOOK

THE KETO KIDS
COOKBOOK

LOW-CARB, HIGH-FAT MEALS
Your Whole Family Will Love!

SAM DILLARD

Author of *The "I Love My Air Fryer" Keto Diet Recipe Book*
and founder of Hey Keto Mama

PAGE STREET
PUBLISHING CO.

PAGE STREET
PUBLISHING CO.

THIS BOOK IS DEDICATED TO

MY TWO LITTLE ONES, JOEY AND MAYA,
AS WELL AS KETO KIDS EVERYWHERE.

CONTENTS

INTRODUCTION

Are you ready to transform your family's way of eating? Transitioning your family to a Ketogenic diet is a very manageable switch worth your consideration, and this collection of recipes is your guide.

At their core, these recipes are made with real food—protein, healthy fats and nutrient-dense vegetables. These are meals the entire family can enjoy and adapt to personal tastes.

Three years ago, I decided to transition to a Ketogenic diet. I wanted something that was sustainable for myself and didn't make me feel as though I couldn't enjoy my favorite foods. As I first read about Keto, it became clear this was a lifestyle change I could make long term. Through this way of eating, I went from feeling low energy and constantly craving food to understanding what my body really needed. I feel more connected to my body and aware of my overall health.

The process of transitioning my family's eating habits meant I started to experiment in the kitchen more. My son was a year old at the time and didn't particularly care for vegetables, as many kids don't. I always felt Keto was easier to manage because veggies are carbs—the smallest food group to focus on. Rather than feel concerned I wasn't feeding my family enough variety, I focused on a few very nutrient-dense vegetables. These were easier to incorporate into many savory, fat-focused dishes.

I began writing recipes and sharing them with others online and soon started my blog, Hey Keto Mama. The blog has given me so much purpose and has allowed me to forge strong connections with others following the Keto diet, more so than I had ever imagined. Some of the most significant connections are with those who comment that I've helped them stay on track with weight loss when they felt like giving up, or have stories of their children with serious illnesses being treated by low-carb or Ketogenic diets. Those who can finally enjoy a delicious cake for a special occasion and be in the moment, rather than focus on what they can't have, are my motivation to keep testing and creating.

One of my favorite things about eating Keto is how sustainable it is as a lifestyle. Critics may say it's too hard to keep up with or that the food choices are too limited, but my readers show me every day how achievable it can be as long as you take it one day at a time. I've seen firsthand how the Ketogenic diet can change lives for the better, and through this book, I hope to get you excited and comfortable knowing that we're all in this together, taking it one day at a time.

KETO BASICS

So, why would a kid follow a Ketogenic diet? There are many reasons, such as managing health conditions under a doctor's orders, maintaining a healthy weight or even because they're following a healthier lifestyle alongside their parents. Each meal is an opportunity to encourage healthy food choices.

Always be sure to discuss any lifestyle changes or health concerns with your family doctor.

As you may already know, the Ketogenic, or Keto, diet is focused around eating minimal carbohydrates, moderate protein and high fat. The goal is to have carbs make up about 5 percent of your daily calories, protein about 25 percent and fat about 70 percent.

By limiting the amount of carbs your body takes in, and focusing instead on rich proteins (like chicken, beef or salmon) and healthy fats (like avocado, cheese and almonds), your body can enter a state of ketosis—not to be confused with ketoacidosis, which is a complication of diabetes.

When the body is in short supply of glucose (which comes from carbs), ketones are made in the liver from the breakdown of fats through a process called ketosis.

Ketosis super-charges your mind and body so you can feel your absolute best, and the Keto lifestyle helps you to develop a healthy relationship with food, so you know what you should be feeding yourself and why.

Because everybody and every body is different, there is no mandatory set of rules to follow. Do what works for you and your family, and feel free to adjust regularly and try new things throughout your journey. This will be an important key to success.

NET CARBS

The nutrition question I'm asked most frequently is, "What are net carbs, and how do I calculate them?"

Many followers of Keto prefer to track net carbs instead of total carbs. Net carbs are total carbs minus dietary fiber and sugar alcohols. Tracking net carbs is generally allowed within the diet because of how your body reacts to the fiber and sugar alcohols in the foods you eat.

On nutrition labels, the grams of dietary fiber and sugar alcohols are already included in the total carb count. Fiber and low-glycemic sugar alcohols, such as erythritol, are carbs that your body can't digest. They have virtually no effect on your blood sugar levels and can be subtracted.

Example: If your food item has 10 grams of carbs for one serving, 6 grams of fiber and 2 grams of erythritol—my favorite natural sweetener—your food item has 2 grams NET carbs per serving.

Some people choose to count total carbs, and that's okay too. Do what works best for you.

HOW TO GET KIDS STARTED ON KETO

Transitioning to a new way of eating may feel intimidating to your kids, but there's a lot you can do to make things easier for everyone. Remember, it may take trying new foods multiple times before a kid accepts them, but don't let that discourage you. Here are some tips that will help make the transition smoother.

START SLOW: Quitting carbs cold turkey isn't recommended because it can make the food temptations come back hard and fast. Instead, try to gradually introduce lower carb and more nutritious substitutions, while slowly phasing out old favorites.

COMBAT CRAVINGS: When cutting back on carbs, especially sugar, the first couple of weeks can be difficult when it comes to craving old carby foods. In my personal experience, it takes about two weeks for the cravings to decrease dramatically. While finding fun recipes can help keep the peace in your family, sometimes getting more active and doing fun nonfood activities is one of the best ways to combat cravings. Extra trips to the park, doing crafts together and even picking out a special recipe together when it is time to eat will help keep your kids' minds off sugar.

COOK TOGETHER: Cooking together is a great way to educate the whole family on what we should be putting into our bodies and why. Even from a young age, kids can become familiar with nutritious ingredients. Being involved in the cooking process can help foster healthy relationships with those better-for-you foods.

PUT SOME CHEESE ON IT: When the little ones' plates just aren't getting cleaned, add cheese. Cheese is a nutritious, very low-carb saving grace to help make even the toughest foods more appealing. It's totally Keto-friendly and has plenty of fat to help keep everyone feeling fuller.

DRINK A LOT OF WATER: Electrolyte and water needs increase on a Ketogenic diet, and sodium, magnesium and potassium specifically are important to watch. When starting Keto, lack of these can cause the headaches or sluggishness you may have heard about—referred to as "Keto flu." The great thing is this is totally avoidable! Encourage the kids to drink even more water than usual to be sure they're staying properly hydrated, and turn to tasty electrolyte powders or drops to add to drinks— I like Keto Chow Fasting Drops—or pick up capsule supplements that will keep bodies in balance.

BE PATIENT: Changing the way your child eats is difficult, and the most important thing is that you're patient with the process. If they're resisting veggies or new textures, keep trying. You may find they just don't enjoy some textures or flavors, and that's okay. Keep exploring and embrace the foods they do enjoy, while slowly introducing new ones.

PANTRY STAPLES FOR A KETO KITCHEN

As you begin to build your new Keto-friendly pantry, here are some basics that will help you get started.

SUGAR ALTERNATIVES: If you have a sweet tooth, you'll definitely want to make some low-carb goodies that don't include sugar. My favorite natural sugar substitute is called erythritol. Two popular brands are Swerve and SoNourished, and erythritol comes in granular and powdered form, just like sugar! I use erythritol in these recipes because it's what appeals to my personal tastes. If you prefer a different sweetener like Stevia or monk fruit, feel free to use those but be aware you'll need to adjust the amount.

ALMOND FLOUR/COCONUT FLOUR: These are two of the most common flours used in low-carb recipes. They aren't equal 1:1 if you're substituting; coconut flour is much more absorbent than almond flour and only requires one-third of the amount per cup of almond flour. Both are more expensive than wheat flour, but shopping at bulk stores can help bring down the cost, especially if you're cooking with them frequently. I use blanched, finely ground almond flour for the recipes in this book, because I've found that it produces the best results in terms of rise and taste. Bob's Red Mill and King Arthur are two brands with excellent-quality almond flours.

ALMOND BUTTER: You'd never believe almond butter is as versatile as it is! Not only is it delicious off the spoon, but it makes a great base in cookies. Even a spoonful or two can make a huge difference in a recipe. I find it adds a depth in flavor that sometimes almond flour alone can't achieve.

PROTEIN POWDER: Protein powder is for more than just shakes. It can help add balance to a recipe's macros, or it can be used as a flour or to add flavor to a recipe. As a parent, I find protein powder helpful to give the kids a little extra boost, especially if you have a picky eater who doesn't love meat.

XANTHAN GUM: Thickeners like xanthan gum are helpful for many types of recipes. It can thicken soups, give baked goods more structure and make sauces extra thick and creamy. It's usually found in the baking aisle and comes in both larger bags and smaller packets. Buying a few smaller packets at a time is a great option when you're just beginning to experiment with it.

Whether you're managing your child's health condition or simply want to change your family's lifestyle, in this book you'll find resources and tips to help you make a smooth transition. Remember, you may need to try several times to get the little ones to enjoy a new food, but don't be discouraged. You're making an important change for the best that your family will benefit from their whole lives.

Let's get started!

RESTAURANT FAVORITES

WHEN DINING OUT, it can be really hard to find low-carb restaurant options that are fit for a kid's taste buds. Kid menus all seem to have the same (few) options, and they're often lower quality or not as freshly made as you may hope. The recipes in this chapter give your kids those restaurant flavors they crave, they come together quickly and the best part is that you know exactly what's in them! Preparing a restaurant-style dinner for your family without spending too much time in the kitchen on busy nights will leave you feeling like you're a superhero.

Make an event out of these meals by breaking out the special plates and creating your own kid's restaurant choice at home. Have the kiddos dress up as chefs, create a silly centerpiece and put on their favorite music.

This chapter will take care of all of your kids' restaurant cravings with simple recipes from Finger Lickin' Fried Chicken (page 16) to a piled-high Turkey Kids Club (page 23)—yes, Keto-friendly sandwiches!

FINGER LICKIN' FRIED CHICKEN

This recipe has all the crunch of traditional fried chicken but uses pork rinds and almond flour instead of the typical white flour and bread crumbs "breading." The kids will love this meal because the seasoning takes plain chicken up a notch but doesn't have any overwhelming flavors. You can also use an air fryer to cook this meal, if you have one. The temperature and cook time will be the same, but make sure to flip the chicken after about 12 minutes.

Serves: 4

1 tsp paprika

¼ tsp garlic powder

¼ tsp onion powder

¼ tsp dried oregano

¼ tsp dried thyme

Salt and pepper, to taste, optional

4 (6-oz [170-g]) chicken breasts, split lengthwise

¼ cup (58 g) mayo

2 oz (57 g) plain pork rinds, crushed

¼ cup (28 g) blanched, finely ground almond flour

Your favorite dipping sauce, for serving

Preheat the oven to 375°F (190°C), line a large baking sheet with parchment and place a rack on top of the parchment.

In a small bowl, mix the paprika, garlic powder, onion powder, oregano and thyme. Add your preferred amount of salt and pepper, if desired. Sprinkle the chicken with the seasoning on both sides.

Gently spread a thin layer of mayo onto each piece of chicken. In a large bowl or plate, mix the pork rinds and almond flour together. Coat each piece of chicken with the pork rind mixture evenly on both sides.

Place each piece of chicken onto the prepared baking sheet. Place the baking sheet into the oven and cook for 25 minutes, or until the internal temperature of the chicken reaches at least 165°F (75°C) and the coating is golden brown.

Serve warm with your favorite dipping sauce.

PER SERVING: 375 Calories, 2.9 g Total Carbs, 1 g Fiber, 1.9 g Net Carbs, 45 g Protein, 19.6 g Fat

CLASSIC BEEF SLIDERS

Burgers are always a hit with the family, and they're so easy to make that you can have dinner on the table in no time. The kids will love these, because they're covered in melty cheese and made with their little hands in mind. Since sliders are smaller than regular burgers, these will cook up on the stovetop in just minutes. This recipe uses pork rinds as a binder, but don't worry if they aren't your thing; you can swap them for equal amounts almond flour or grated Parmesan cheese.

Serves: 6

1 lb (454 g) 80/20 ground beef

1 egg

1 tsp Worcestershire sauce

¼ tsp garlic powder

¼ tsp ground black pepper

½ oz (14 g) finely ground pork rinds

1 tbsp (14 g) coconut oil

6 Magical Keto Rolls (page 59)

3 slices mild cheddar, cut in half

6 tbsp (84 g) Burger Sauce (page 181), optional, for serving

6 lettuce leaves

In a large bowl, mix the ground beef, egg, Worcestershire, garlic powder, pepper and pork rinds. Form the mixture into six small patties.

In a pan over medium heat, melt the coconut oil. When the oil is hot and crackling, sear each burger for approximately 45 seconds to 1 minute per side. Lower the heat and cook for 3 to 5 minutes to your preferred doneness.

To build the burgers, place a beef slider on each Keto roll and top with cheddar, burger sauce (if desired) and lettuce. Serve warm.

KIDS, YOU CAN HELP!
Once the burgers are done cooking, ask your grown-up to let you help decorate the burgers. Top them with cheese, burger sauce, lettuce and any of your other absolute favorite toppings!

PER SERVING: 631 Calories, 10.5 g Total Carbs, 3.7 g Fiber, 6.7 g Net Carbs, 29.3 g Protein, 52.2 g Fat

JICAMA FRIES

Fries are always a kid favorite. Just because potatoes are high in carbs doesn't mean the little ones can't enjoy their beloved crispy fries. Jicama fries take on the flavor of whatever seasoning you use, which makes them really unique. Jicama is a large root vegetable that's sometimes referred to as a Mexican potato. When you cut into a jicama, you can expect to see what looks like a white potato. Although it looks like a potato, the taste is lightly sweet. These fries are a healthier alternative that you'll be surprised you didn't try sooner.

Serves: 6

1 medium jicama, peeled and cut into ¼-inch (6-mm)-thick sticks

2 tbsp (30 ml) melted coconut oil

½ tsp paprika

¼ tsp garlic powder

¼ tsp ground black pepper

Salt, optional

Your favorite dipping sauce, for serving

Preheat the oven to 400°F (200°C). Line a large baking sheet with parchment.

In a large bowl, toss the jicama sticks in the coconut oil. Place the jicama sticks onto the baking sheet. Sprinkle each side of the sticks with the paprika, garlic powder and pepper.

Bake for 12 minutes. Flip them over and bake for 13 minutes or until they turn golden at the edges and begin to crisp.

Sprinkle them with salt, if desired.

Serve warm with your favorite dipping sauce, such as Classic Ketchup (page 166) or Burger Sauce (page 181).

MAKE IT YOUR OWN!
Since these fries take on the seasoning you use, feel free to add your favorite! Just swap the seasoning for a teaspoon of your favorite Italian herb blend, taco seasoning or even dry ranch seasoning for a zesty kick!

PER SERVING: 81 Calories, 9.9 g Total Carbs, 5.4 g Fiber, 4.4 g Net Carbs, 0.8 g Protein, 4.7 g Fat

TURKEY KIDS CLUB

Sandwiches are the best. They're fast, portable, customizable and, of course, incredibly delicious. You might have thought your days of sinking your teeth into a mouthwatering sandwich were done, but with this recipe, those days are just getting started. Since bread is always a favorite with kids, this club uses a flatbread made from Keto-friendly ingredients that make it taste like the regular sandwiches they love. This Turkey Kids Club is the perfect fresh and nutritious meal, but the possibilities for making this your own are endless!

Serves: 4

Flatbread
1 cup (112 g) shredded mozzarella cheese

1 oz (28 g) cream cheese

¾ cup (84 g) blanched, finely ground almond flour

¼ cup (26 g) ground golden flax

1 egg

½ tsp baking soda

Filling
8 oz (227 g) sliced deli turkey breast

4 slices cooked sugar-free bacon

4 leaves Bibb lettuce

½ Roma tomato, cut into 4 slices

Preheat the oven to 350°F (180°C) and line a large baking sheet with parchment.

In a large microwave-safe mixing bowl, add the mozzarella and cream cheese. Break the cream cheese into bits, and add the almond flour. Microwave for 1 minute and then stir until a soft dough ball forms.

Add the flax and egg and sprinkle with baking soda. Stir until the egg is fully incorporated and a soft dough forms.

Wet your hands and, on the parchment-lined baking sheet, press the dough flat into a large rectangle, about ¼ inch (0.6 cm) thick.

Bake it for 10 to 12 minutes, or until it begins to turn golden brown. Let it cool for at least 15 minutes before cutting it into eight rectangles.

Place four of the flatbread rectangles on a work surface and top each with 2 ounces (57 g) of turkey and one slice of bacon, broken in half.

Add a lettuce leaf and a slice of tomato to each. Place the other flatbread rectangles on top of the tomato to complete the sandwiches. Serve immediately or wrap in cling wrap and store in the fridge for up to 2 days.

PER SERVING: 412 Calories, 12.5 g Total Carbs, 3.7 g Fiber, 8.7 g Net Carbs, 32.5 g Protein, 25.9 g Fat

CHICKEN-CAULIFLOWER FRIED RICE

Chicken-Cauliflower Fried Rice is a great recipe for the kids, because it's an easy way to get your veggies and protein. This meal makes a great lunch on those days where you're running behind schedule, the kids are hungry and you need to prepare something quick and flavorful. Kids will love this because it has all the traditional flavors of take-out fried rice, and you can customize it by adding more of their favorite veggies or meat, if you prefer.

Serves: 4

1 large head cauliflower

2 tbsp (28 g) coconut oil

¼ cup (40 g) chopped white onion

1 cup (90 g) chopped broccoli

2 cups (250 g) cooked, cubed chicken thighs

2 tbsp (30 ml) soy sauce or liquid aminos

¼ tsp garlic powder

¼ tsp ground ginger

1 large egg

2 green onions, sliced

Remove the leaves and stems from the cauliflower. Cut the cauliflower into florets and place into a food processor. Pulse 5 to 10 times or until the cauliflower resembles rice.

In a large skillet, melt the coconut oil over medium heat. Place the riced cauliflower, white onion and broccoli into the skillet and cover and cook for 5 minutes.

Remove the lid and stir the vegetables. Cook until the broccoli and cauliflower are tender, about 5 to 10 minutes. Add the cooked chicken to the pan and pour in the soy sauce, garlic powder and ginger.

Gently mix the cauliflower rice until all is coated with the soy sauce. Push the cauliflower rice, chicken, onion and broccoli to the edges of the pan and crack open the egg into the center of the pan.

Let the egg fry for about 1 to 2 minutes until it's firm, then chop it with your spatula and gently fold into the rest of the rice. Top with sliced green onions and serve warm.

KIDS, YOU CAN HELP!
With the help of your grown-up, you can run the food processor to make the rice! This is a fun and easy way to help out with dinner!

PER SERVING: 427 Calories, 13.1 g Total Carbs, 4.9 g Fiber, 8.1 g Net Carbs, 15.9 g Protein, 36.2 g Fat

ITALIAN SUB IN A TUB

Sandwiches are one of the easiest convenience foods. Kids will love this meal because it has more of their favorite parts of the sandwich—the inside! This bowl is packed with more meat and cheese than a typical salad would have, so kids will be full for longer. Many sandwich shops will offer their subs in a bowl, and while tasty, they're usually still the same cost as a whole sandwich. This meal has all the same flavor and is more cost effective. Plus, the kids will love adding the toppings to their own bowl!

Serves: 2

3 cups (141 g) shredded romaine lettuce

4 oz (113 g) genoa salami, sliced into strips

4 oz (113 g) chopped deli ham

2 slices provolone cheese, sliced into strips

1 Roma tomato, diced

2 tbsp (30 ml) olive oil

2 tsp (10 ml) apple cider vinegar

¼ tsp oregano

¼ tsp ground black pepper

Place the lettuce into a large bowl. Add the salami, ham, provolone and tomato. Gently toss everything.

In a small bowl, mix the olive oil, apple cider vinegar, oregano and pepper. Drizzle the mixture over the meat and lettuce and toss to coat. Separate into two servings and enjoy immediately.

MEAL PREP!
Make this dish ahead of time for a quick meal during the week. Simply don't add the olive oil and vinegar dressing until you're ready to eat. Store it in the fridge in an airtight container for up to 4 days for maximum freshness.

PER SERVING: 405 Calories, 10.5 g Total Carbs, 3.3 g Fiber, 7.2 g Net Carbs, 20.1 g Protein, 31.8 g Fat

CHEESE SHELL TACOS

Cheese is arguably the best part of tacos anyway . . . why not flip the script and skip the carby tortillas completely by making the shells out of cheese? You won't miss tortillas at all once you're biting into delicious and crispy cheese! Everyone will have a blast loading up their shells with all the healthy fats in sour cream and guacamole, and they'll stay full and energized for the rest of the day.

Yield: 8 cheese shell tacos, 2 per serving

½ lb (227 g) ground beef

1 tbsp (6 g) chili powder

2 tsp (4 g) ground cumin

¼ tsp garlic powder

2⅔ cups (304 g) shredded mild cheddar cheese

½ cup (120 g) salsa

¼ cup (60 g) sour cream

¼ cup (60 g) Restaurant-Style Guacamole (page 178)

Preheat the oven to 400°F (200°C) and line two large baking sheets with parchment.

In a large skillet, brown the ground beef until no pink remains, about 10 minutes, then drain the grease from the pan. Return the pan to the heat, add the chili powder, ground cumin and garlic powder, and cook for 3 minutes. Set aside and keep warm.

Place ⅓-cup (38-g) mounds of cheese on the baking sheets, leaving a few inches between each mound.

Place the sheets into the oven and bake for 8 to 10 minutes, or until the cheese begins to turn golden and is completely melted. Remove the trays from the oven and allow the cheese to cool for 5 minutes.

Place a couple of spoonfuls of meat onto each taco and fold the cheese over the top. Serve with salsa, sour cream and guacamole for dipping. Feel free to add your favorite taco fillings, such as shredded lettuce and tomato.

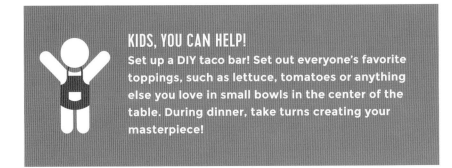

KIDS, YOU CAN HELP!
Set up a DIY taco bar! Set out everyone's favorite toppings, such as lettuce, tomatoes or anything else you love in small bowls in the center of the table. During dinner, take turns creating your masterpiece!

PER SERVING: 569 Calories, 8.2 g Total Carbs, 3 g Fiber, 5.2 g Net Carbs, 28 g Protein, 47.4 g Fat

HOMEMADE TORTILLAS

Pork rinds in tortillas may sound a bit odd, but when ground down, pork rinds make a great flour alternative! There's a high demand in the Keto community for easy and plain tortillas. Oftentimes, I've found that many require difficult-to-find ingredients or lack flavor. The flavor from the pork rinds makes these tortillas a delicious alternative. These can be used in a variety of ways, including for breakfast burritos, quesadillas or sandwich wraps. Use the nutrition info for these tortillas as a base, and then enjoy adding your favorite toppings. Kids will love these because they fry up extra crunchy!

Yield: 4 small tortillas

½ cup (56 g) shredded mozzarella cheese

2 oz (56 g) cream cheese

1 oz (28 g) finely crushed pork rinds

1 egg

1 tbsp (14 g) coconut oil

Set out a cooling rack.

Place the mozzarella cheese in a large microwave-safe bowl. Break the cream cheese into bits and toss it in with the mozzarella. Microwave for 30 to 45 seconds or until the cheese is melted and can be stirred into a smooth ball.

Add the pork rinds and egg. Stir until a soft ball of dough forms.

Place the dough between two pieces of parchment paper and roll into a large circle, ¼ inch (6 mm) thick. Cut out 4½-inch (11.4-cm) circles from the dough.

In a skillet over medium heat, warm the coconut oil until sizzling. Fry each tortilla for 3 to 5 minutes on each side until it begins to turn golden brown. Place on the cooling rack or serve immediately.

DOUBLE IT!
You can easily double this recipe for twice as many delicious mini tacos or even four large ones for the grown-ups to enjoy.

PER SERVING: 151 Calories, 0.8 g Total Carbs, 0 g Fiber, 0.8 g Net Carbs, 10 g Protein, 11.8 g Fat

CLASSICS EVERY KID CRAVES

YOU CAN'T BEAT THE CLASSICS. This chapter is loaded with the best low-carb swaps for all of your kids' favorite meals. Forget about foods you'd find in the freezer section. Every recipe in this chapter is quick, fun . . . and actually good for you!

These recipes define childhood and what it means to be a kid, and just because you're on a low-carb lifestyle, that doesn't mean you have to miss out!

Who doesn't love mac and cheese (page 39), chicken nuggets (page 36) and, of course, my personal favorite . . . PIZZA (page 35)! This chapter has it all, along with fun tips to add your own personal kidilicious spin to all your faves!

PERFECT PEPPERONI PIZZA

What kid doesn't love pizza night? This crust is packed with enough fat and protein to be filling but without all the carbs that leave everyone feeling sluggish. The crust is made with a cheese-based dough that can be a little tough to work with the first time, but it doesn't take long to become your absolute favorite versatile dough! It can make pizza, calzones and even desserts. Just be sure to wet your hands before handling it to prevent sticking.

Yield: 8 slices, 2 per serving

1½ cups (170 g) shredded mozzarella cheese

2 oz (56 g) cream cheese

½ cup (56 g) blanched, finely ground almond flour

1 egg

½ tsp baking powder

¼ cup (63 g) marinara sauce, plus more for dipping, optional

½ cup (56 g) shredded mild cheddar cheese

10 slices pepperoni

2 tbsp (10 g) grated Parmesan cheese

Mouthwatering Marinara (page 170) or Rockin' Ranch Dip (page 174) for dipping, optional

Preheat the oven to 400°F (200°C). Line a baking sheet with parchment.

In a large microwave-safe bowl, combine the mozzarella, cream cheese and almond flour. Microwave for 1 minute. Stir it until a soft dough ball forms, and then add the egg and baking powder.

Press the dough ball into a ¼-inch (6-mm)-thick, 12-inch (30.5-cm) circle on the prepared baking sheet. Bake for 5 minutes.

Remove and spoon the marinara sauce over the crust. Sprinkle with cheddar, and place the pepperoni around the pizza. Return it to the oven and bake for 15 minutes, or until the crust is golden and the cheese is bubbling and browned.

Let it cool for 10 minutes before slicing and serving, then sprinkle with Parmesan. Serve with marinara sauce or ranch dressing for dipping, if desired.

KIDS, YOU CAN HELP!
Make pizza night even more fun by making mini pizzas with silly faces! Decorate your pizza with your favorite toppings, making the funniest faces you can think of. After they're done baking, give them silly Parmesan hair!

PER SERVING: 387 Calories, 10.3 g Total Carbs, 2.2 g Fiber, 8 g Net Carbs, 23 g Protein, 28.5 g Fat

OVEN-BAKED CHICKEN NUGGETS

Sometimes it seems like chicken nuggets are their own food group to kids. Whether they're fried or baked, the flour coating still usually contains too many carbs to easily fit into a Ketogenic diet. These baked chicken nuggets are made from ground chicken thigh, which is juicy and flavorful. If you can't find ground chicken at the store, you can place boneless, skinless chicken thighs in your food processor and pulse a few times until it's the right consistency. You can also ask your local butcher to grind some up for you fresh! The nuggets are coated in almond flour and pork rinds for a super crunch rivaling that of regular nuggets. This recipe takes a little effort but is absolutely worth it for the little ones!

Yield: 20 nuggets, 4 per serving

1 lb (454 g) ground chicken thigh

¼ cup (20 g) grated Parmesan cheese

½ cup (56 g) shredded cheddar cheese

½ cup (56 g) blanched, finely ground almond flour

1 egg

1 oz (28 g) finely ground pork rinds

Classic Ketchup (page 166) or BBQ Sauce (page 169), for dipping

Preheat the oven to 375°F (190°C). Line two baking sheets with parchment.

In a large bowl, mix the chicken, Parmesan and cheddar cheeses.

Take 2 tablespoons (22 g) of the mixture and form it into a chicken nugget shape, round and thick, about ½ inch (1.3 cm) high.

Place the nuggets on one of the baking sheets and freeze for 20 minutes.

In a medium bowl, place the almond flour. In a separate medium bowl, whisk the egg. In another medium bowl, place the pork rinds.

Remove the nuggets from the freezer and dip a nugget into the egg. Shake to remove the excess, then press it into the almond flour. Dip it back into the egg, and then press it into the crushed pork rinds to evenly coat.

Place the nuggets on the second baking sheet. Bake for 25 minutes or until the outside begins turning golden and the internal temperature is at least 165°F (75°C).

Serve warm with your choice of dipping sauce.

PER SERVING: 500 Calories, 5 g Total Carbs, 1.5 g Fiber, 3.5 g Net Carbs, 29.2 g Protein, 40.2 g Fat

ULTIMATE "MAC" AND CHEESE

For kids, mac and cheese is the best comfort food. There's nothing better than sticking your fork in that warm, gooey cheese until your plate is clean! The traditional dish uses macaroni noodles, which are loaded with carbs (78 grams in just 1 cup!). Cauliflower is an excellent substitute with a delicious taste and plenty of nutrients to keep your body happy. The kids will fall in love with this dish because of the cauliflower's muted taste and the explosion of delicious cheesy flavor!

Serves: 6

1 large head cauliflower

2 cups (480 ml) water

2 tbsp (28 g) butter

¼ cup (40 g) diced yellow onion

½ tsp minced garlic

½ cup (120 ml) heavy whipping cream

2 oz (56 g) softened cream cheese

1½ cups (170 g) shredded sharp cheddar cheese

1 oz (28 g) finely ground pork rinds

¼ cup (20 g) grated Parmesan

DON'T LIKE PORK RINDS?
No problem! You can leave the pork rinds out, if you don't mind not having a crunchy topping. You can also try crushing cheese crisps, such as Whisps or Parm Crisps, and using those in place of the pork rinds.

Preheat the oven to 400°F (200°C) and prepare a 9 x 9-inch (23 x 23–cm) baking dish with nonstick cooking spray.

Remove the leaves from the cauliflower and cut it into florets. Pour the water into a large pot over medium heat. Place a steamer basket into the pot, and bring the water to a boil.

Place the cauliflower florets into the steamer basket, or directly into the water if you do not have a steamer basket.

Cover the pot and let the cauliflower steam for 11 to 15 minutes, or until it's tender. Remove from the heat and allow to cool. Place the cooked florets into a bowl of ice water to cool faster, if desired.

Using a clean kitchen towel or cheese cloth, wring out as much water as you can from the cauliflower. Place it in a bowl and set aside.

In a large saucepan over medium heat, melt the butter. Add the onion and sauté until it begins to soften, about 3 to 5 minutes. Add the garlic and stir until fragrant, about 30 seconds.

Pour the heavy whipping cream into the pan and add the cream cheese. Whisk until smooth. Turn off the heat and add the cheddar. Using a rubber spatula or spoon, stir the mixture until the cheese is completely melted and smooth.

Add the cauliflower into the pot and fold it into the cheese mixture until it's fully coated. Pour the mixture into the prepared baking dish and top with pork rinds and Parmesan.

Bake for 20 minutes, or until bubbling and golden brown.

PER SERVING: 497 Calories, 13.3 g Total Carbs, 4.4 g Fiber, 8.9 g Net Carbs, 22.7 g Protein, 40.6 g Fat

HAM AND CHEESE WAFFLES

Ham and cheese is pretty simple on its own, but it gets even easier when you mix up the ingredients and pour them on a waffle iron! This creates a gooey, savory waffle with that classic ham and cheese sandwich taste in every bite. All of this for just a fraction of the carbs of the original! These waffles make a great snack or quick lunch when you're on the go. You can even make them ahead of time and store them in an airtight container in the fridge. Just pop them in the microwave for 30 seconds before eating and you'll be good to go!

Yield: 4 (4-inch [10-cm]) waffles, 1 per serving

1 cup (112 g) shredded mozzarella cheese

¼ cup (20 g) grated Parmesan cheese

1 egg

½ cup (56 g) diced ham

Preheat a waffle iron.

In a large bowl, mix the mozzarella, Parmesan, egg and ham. Place about a quarter of the mixture onto the center of the waffle iron. It won't fill to the edges, and that's okay.

Let the waffle cook for 5 to 7 minutes, depending on your waffle iron. The waffles will be dark golden brown and crispy when finished. Use a fork to carefully remove the waffles from the iron and allow them to cool for at least 5 minutes. Cooling will allow them to firm up but still be gooey inside like a grilled ham and cheese sandwich.

MAKE IT YOUR OWN!
Feel free to swap out the ham and use your own favorite add-ins. Chopped pepperoni makes a yummy pizza waffle alongside some Mouthwatering Marinara (page 170) for dipping.

PER SERVING: 148 Calories, 2.2 g Total Carbs, 0 g Fiber, 2.2 g Net Carbs, 15.2 g Protein, 8.4 g Fat

HIDDEN VEGGIE SLOPPY JOEYS

If your kid is anything like my son, Joey, they don't like actually seeing veggies in their food. It's not that he minds them being there. He loves spinach in smoothies, but to actually look at it while he eats—nope! There are lots of veggies hidden in this meal, but you wouldn't know it. The classic flavors are all there but hidden in the deep red sauce and meat. If your little ones are still a little resistant, try adding melted cheese on top. That was my favorite way to eat them as a kid!

Serves: 4

½ cup (124 g) no-sugar-added tomato sauce

1 tbsp (16 g) tomato paste

¼ cup (40 g) diced yellow onion

½ chopped green bell pepper

½ tsp Worcestershire sauce

1 lb (454 g) 80/20 ground beef

2 tbsp (28 g) butter

¼ tsp garlic powder

¼ tsp chili powder

1 tsp apple cider vinegar

Lettuce leaves, Magical Keto Rolls (page 59) or zucchini noodles, for serving

Pour the tomato sauce into a food processor and add the tomato paste, onion, bell pepper and Worcestershire sauce. Pulse until most of the veggies are pureed. If you prefer a chunky texture, pulse fewer times or feel free to skip this step.

In a skillet over medium-high heat, brown the ground beef until no pink remains, about 7 to 10 minutes. Drain the grease from the pan and replace the pan and the meat over the heat.

Place the butter into the pan with the beef and add the garlic powder, chili powder and vinegar. Pour in the veggie sauce. Stir until all the meat is coated. Let it simmer for 10 minutes. Serve with lettuce leaves, on Magical Keto Rolls (page 59) or over zucchini noodles.

PER SERVING: 363 Calories, 4.2 g Total Carbs, 0.9 g Fiber, 3.2 g Net Carbs, 20.9 g Protein, 28.8 g Fat

TURKEY AND ZUCCHINI MEATBALLS

Meatballs are a childhood favorite. The kids will love these hidden-veggie meatballs, because they're savory and bursting with cheesy goodness. These meatballs use ground turkey for a lighter flavor than traditional beef. While it's true that turkey is leaner than ground beef, it still has a good amount of fat. Some extra lean turkey has most of it removed, but others have around 18 grams of fat per 4-ounce (115-g) serving. That's pretty good! Lower amounts of fat can sometimes be helpful when making food for the kiddos or if you're watching your calories. Enjoy these meatballs by themselves or bake them into a casserole covered in Mouthwatering Marinara (page 170).

Yield: 20 meatballs, 4 per serving

1 medium zucchini, shredded

1 lb (454 g) ground turkey

1 egg

½ cup (56 g) shredded mozzarella cheese

½ cup (40 g) grated Parmesan cheese

½ tsp dried parsley

¼ tsp dried oregano

¼ tsp ground black pepper

¼ tsp garlic powder

Preheat the oven to 375°F (190°C) and line a large baking sheet with parchment.

Place the shredded zucchini into a clean kitchen towel or cheese cloth and wring out as much excess moisture as possible.

Place the zucchini into a large bowl and add the turkey, egg, mozzarella, Parmesan, parsley, oregano, pepper and garlic powder.

Roll the mixture into 20 balls, each one about 2 inches (5 cm) wide. Place the meatballs on the baking sheet and bake for 25 minutes or until fully cooked through. Serve warm.

MAKE IT A CASSEROLE
Place the cooked meatballs into an 8 x 8-inch (20 x 20-cm) baking dish. Pour ½ cup (120 ml) of Mouthwatering Marinara (page 170) over them and sprinkle with a little cheese. Place them into the oven and broil for 3 to 5 minutes or until the cheese is browned and bubbling.

PER SERVING: 329 Calories, 3.3 g Total Carbs, 0.6 g Fiber, 2.7 g Net Carbs, 37.1 g Protein, 18.3 g Fat

MAYA'S MEATLOAF

This twist on a classic meatloaf is so yummy, even my two-year-old, Maya, gobbles it right up! It's made by mixing ground beef with a Mexican-style pork sausage called chorizo. The spices in the chorizo create a flavor-filled twist on the classic meatloaf dish. You won't find a sugary glaze like in most meatloaf recipes—I let the real flavors speak for themselves in this family-friendly dish! If you do enjoy a glaze, try Classic Ketchup (page 166) or BBQ Sauce (page 169) sweetened with a Keto-friendly sweetener, such as Stevia or erythritol.

Serves: 6

1 lb (454 g) ground beef

½ lb (226 g) ground Mexican chorizo

¼ cup (40 g) chopped yellow onion

¼ cup (22 g) chopped jalapeños

2 tbsp (2 g) chopped fresh cilantro

½ cup (28 g) ground pork rinds

1 egg

½ tsp garlic powder

½ tsp dried oregano

1 tsp chili powder

1 tsp salt

Preheat the oven to 400°F (200°C). Spray a 5 x 9–inch (13 x 23–cm) loaf pan with nonstick cooking spray.

In a large mixing bowl, combine the ground beef, chorizo, onion, jalapeños, cilantro, pork rinds, egg, garlic powder, oregano, chili powder and salt. Fold together until fully combined. Form the meat mixture into a loaf shape and place it in the loaf pan.

Bake for 40 minutes or until the top is browned, the center is no longer pink and it has reached an internal temperature of at least 160°F (70°C).

THE BEST BREADCRUMB SUBSTITUTE

Breadcrumbs act as a binder in many meatloaf recipes, but they add unnecessary carbs. Pork rinds have zero carbs and are a great swap to keep your meal Keto. To make ground pork rinds, just place them into your food processor and pulse until they resemble a fine breading. It's as simple as that!

One ounce (28 g) of pork rinds will make about ½ cup ground.

PER SERVING: 372 Calories, 1.6 g Total Carbs, 0.3 g Fiber, 1.3 g Net Carbs, 22.6 g Protein, 30.6 g Fat

QUICK AND EASY MASHED CAULIFLOWER

Who knew cauliflower was so multitalented? It can stand in for so many of your favorites while still tasting great and packing plenty of vitamins and protein. This recipe will soon become your favorite sub for mashed potatoes, and it goes great with Maya's Meatloaf (page 47)! Feel free to get creative and add your favorite herbs to this dish or even some shredded cheese!

Serves: 4

12 oz (340 g) steamer bag cauliflower

2 tbsp (28 g) cubed butter

¼ cup (20 g) grated Parmesan cheese

¼ tsp oregano

¼ tsp garlic powder

½ tsp parsley

¼ cup (60 ml) Rockin' Ranch Dip (page 174)

Steam the cauliflower according to package instructions. Carefully cut open the bag and place the cauliflower into the food processor.

Add the butter, Parmesan, oregano, garlic powder, parsley and ranch dressing to the food processor and pulse 10 to 20 times until it reaches a mostly smooth consistency. If you prefer a chunkier consistency, just pulse until you reach your preferred texture.

Serve warm.

MAKE IT YOUR OWN!
This recipe is super easy to customize with your favorite flavors. Try adding paprika for a smoky flavor or even your favorite shredded cheese! You can also pulse the mixture only 3 to 5 times to make a cauliflower rice, which works well added to your favorite casserole!

PER SERVING: 149 Calories, 4.7 g Total Carbs, 2 g Fiber, 2.7 g Net Carbs, 4.6 g Protein, 12.9 g Fat

JUST FOR ME GRILLED CHEESE

Most Keto breads take a while to prep and bake, but sometimes you just need something fast. This recipe comes together in less than 10 minutes and doesn't require much prep. All you need is your microwave to make a quick 60-second bread and then a buttered skillet to melt the cheese and make it ooey-gooey delicious! Feel free to add bacon, turkey or even some mashed avocado for an extra boost of fat.

Serves: 1

2 tbsp (28 g) butter, divided

3 tbsp (21 g) blanched, finely ground almond flour

½ tsp baking powder

1 egg

1 slice deli American cheese

In a 4-inch (10-cm) round microwave-safe ramekin, melt 1 tablespoon (14 g) of the butter in the microwave, about 30 seconds. Add the almond flour, baking powder and egg. Mix until combined.

Microwave on high for 1 minute. The bread should be firm to the touch when fully cooked with no visible wet spots. The texture will feel similar to a sponge cake. Let it cool, and then slice in half. Place the cheese between the two pieces of bread.

In a skillet over medium heat, melt the remaining 1 tablespoon (14 g) of butter. Place the sandwich into the pan and toast each side until golden and the cheese has melted, for 3 to 5 minutes per side. Serve warm.

PER SERVING: 504 Calories, 8.4 g Total Carbs, 2.2 g Fiber, 6.1 g Net Carbs, 18.2 g Protein, 43.5 g Fat

COMFORTING CHICKEN ALFREDO

Alfredo sauce is not only delicious but so easy to make! Homemade alfredo is so much more flavorful than store bought and doesn't come with all the preservatives. This recipe is creamy and loaded with chicken flavor. Serve with steamed broccoli or your favorite low-carb noodle substitute, such as zucchini noodles or spaghetti squash.

Serves: 4

1 tbsp (14 g) coconut oil

¼ tsp salt

¼ tsp garlic powder

½ tsp dried parsley

¼ tsp dried oregano

2 (6-oz [170-g]) boneless, skinless chicken breasts, sliced in half lengthwise

¼ cup (60 ml) chicken broth

4 tbsp (56 g) butter

2 oz (56 g) cream cheese

¼ cup (60 ml) heavy whipping cream

¼ tsp ground black pepper

¼ cup (20 g) grated Parmesan

¼ tsp xanthan gum, for thickening, optional

In a large skillet over medium-high heat, melt the coconut oil. Sprinkle the salt, garlic powder, parsley and oregano evenly over each piece of chicken.

When the coconut oil begins to pop, place the chicken into the pan and sear quickly on each side. Reduce the heat and cook for 15 to 20 minutes until the chicken reaches an internal temperature of at least 165°F (75°C).

When the chicken is done, remove and set aside. Do not turn off the heat. Pour the chicken broth into the pan and use a wooden spoon to scrape the brown pieces off the bottom.

Cut the butter and cream cheese into small pieces and place them into the pan. Reduce the heat and cover for 2 minutes. Remove the lid from the pan and quickly whisk in the heavy whipping cream.

Add the pepper and bring the mixture to a boil for 30 seconds, then reduce the heat to low. Sprinkle the Parmesan and xanthan gum, if using, into the sauce and whisk quickly. Let it simmer for 4 to 5 minutes until it begins to thicken up.

Turn off the heat and add the cooked chicken to the sauce. Let it sit for 5 minutes before serving. For kids, feel free to slice up the chicken before adding it back into the sauce.

PER SERVING: 351 Calories, 1.8 g Total Carbs, 0.1 g Fiber, 1.7 g Net Carbs, 23.2 g Protein, 27.9 g Fat

MAKE IT YOUR OWN!
If you love chicken alfredo and pizza, try adding the sauce to your favorite low-carb pizza crust or my Keto flatbread (page 23). Chop up the chicken and some veggies, and sprinkle with cheese!

FISH STICKS

This dish is a staple in our home. The kids love it because it's crispy and dipping it into homemade Tartar Sauce (page 177) really takes the fish to the next level. Feel free to add your favorite seafood seasoning, such as a sprinkle of Old Bay seasoning or even lemon pepper to add even more pep to this dish!

Serves: 4

½ cup (56 g) blanched, finely ground almond flour

1 oz (28 g) finely ground pork rinds

1 egg

1 lb (454 g) cod fillet, cut into 1-inch (2.5-cm)-thick sticks

Tartar Sauce (page 177), for serving

Preheat the oven to 400°F (200°C). Line a large baking sheet with parchment.

In a large bowl, mix the almond flour and pork rinds.

In a separate medium bowl, whisk the egg.

Dip each fish stick into the egg, then gently press into the almond flour and pork rind mixture until each side is coated.

Place the fish sticks onto the prepared baking sheet. Bake for 12 to 15 minutes or until the fish is fully cooked and easily flakes. Serve warm with a side of Tartar Sauce (page 177) for dipping.

FREEZE IT!
To make this meal even faster, prepare it ahead of time and freeze. Simply follow the directions and coat the fish sticks. Instead of baking them, place them on a parchment-lined sheet and freeze for 1 hour. Then remove them and store in a sealed freezer bag. You can easily double or even triple the recipe! To bake, simply add an extra 5 to 7 minutes to the cook time if frozen.

PER SERVING: 224 Calories, 4.6 g Total Carbs, 1.5 g Fiber, 3.2 g Net Carbs, 29.3 g Protein, 9.3 g Fat

CHICKEN AND BACON RANCH PIZZA

Friday night in our house is pizza night. Chicken crust pizza may not taste like traditional flour crust pizza, but the trade-off is that it's loaded with protein and has way more flavor. This recipe is simple and delicious but most importantly, it's a hit with the kids! Feel free to dress it up to your own likings or simply enjoy as is for a yummy pizza night you'll all feel good about.

Serves: 6

1 lb (454 g) ground chicken thigh

½ cup (56 g) shredded mozzarella cheese

¼ cup (60 ml) ranch dressing

½ cup (56 g) shredded Monterey Jack cheese

5 slices (40 g) cooked bacon, crumbled

Preheat the oven to 375°F (190°C). Line a large baking sheet with parchment.

In a large bowl, mix the ground chicken with the mozzarella, and press the raw chicken into a rectangle on the baking sheet, about ½ inch (1.3 cm) thick.

Place the sheet into the oven and bake for 20 minutes.

Remove the baking sheet from the oven and place it on a heat-safe surface. Use a spoon to spread the ranch over the chicken crust and then sprinkle with the Monterey Jack cheese. Return the baking sheet to the oven and cook for 15 minutes, or until the cheese is brown and bubbling.

Top the pizza with bacon and allow it to cool for at least 10 minutes before serving.

HIDDEN VEGGIES
If your kiddos are going through a veggie-resistant phase, you can easily add spinach or shredded and drained zucchini to this crust! They might still notice, but they're less likely to care while they're enjoying creamy ranch, crispy bacon and, of course, cheese!

PER SERVING: 318 Calories, 0.8 g Total Carbs, 0 g Fiber, 0.8 g Net Carbs, 16.9 g Protein, 27.5 g Fat

MAGICAL KETO ROLLS

This bread is my all-time favorite; there's no way I could write this book without including it! While it's not as airy and fluffy as traditional bread, it's certainly the best substitute I've had yet. The flax gives this roll a wheat roll texture and flavor, which makes it unique. This recipe works great as rolls, but you can slice to enjoy as burger buns or for sandwiches or pressed into a flatbread. Don't let the cheese dough intimidate you; it's very easy to make and soon you'll be a pro!

Yield: 6 rolls, 1 per serving

1 cup (112 g) shredded mozzarella cheese

1 oz (28 g) cream cheese

1 cup (112 g) blanched, finely ground almond flour

¼ cup (26 g) ground flaxseed

1 egg

½ tsp baking soda

Preheat the oven to 400°F (200°C) and line a baking sheet with parchment, then set aside.

In a medium microwave-safe bowl, add the mozzarella, cream cheese and almond flour. Microwave for 1 minute, and then stir until a soft ball of dough forms.

Add the flax, egg and baking soda. Wet your hands and separate the dough into six even pieces. Gently roll them into balls.

Place the balls onto the baking sheet and bake for 10 to 12 minutes until the tops and edges begin to turn a golden brown.

Let them cool for at least 10 minutes before serving.

PER SERVING: 205 Calories, 8.2 g Total Carbs, 4 g Fiber, 5.2 g Net Carbs, 12.1 g Protein, 13.8 g Fat

EASY WEEKNIGHT DINNERS

FEEDING YOUR WHOLE FAMILY a Keto-friendly weeknight meal is a breeze with these quick and easy dishes everyone will love . . . especially the kids! No more boring plates—each recipe is bursting with flavor and is just waiting to be gobbled up!

These dinners are simple to make and always great to come back to. They prep easily and can often be made the night before, so busy weeknights don't have to feel so overwhelming.

With recipes like Everything But the Bun Cheeseburger Casserole (page 66) and Swimming Salmon Patties (page 83), you're getting all the protein and healthy fats you need to keep your muscles strong and your tummy full. Even better, your taste buds will smile from the very first bite.

So, set the table and get ready to chow down on some seriously yummy grub!

ZESTY BBQ DRUMSTICKS

Weeknights can be busy, but flavorful meals don't have to take long to assemble! Drumsticks were always my favorite as a kid. Leave the skin on for that extra fat and let it get extra crispy for a big crunch! I love using BBQ sauce because it adds a lot of flavor quickly. If you're not used to cooking drumsticks, don't worry! It's easier than it seems. Pair with cheesy cauliflower for a complete meal!

Yield: 8 drumsticks, 1 per serving

8 skin-on chicken drumsticks

1 tsp chili powder

½ tsp garlic powder

½ tsp paprika

¼ tsp ground black pepper

½ cup (120 ml) BBQ Sauce (page 169), for serving

Preheat the oven to 375°F (190°C). Line a large baking sheet with aluminum foil.

Sprinkle the drumsticks with the chili powder, garlic powder, paprika and pepper, patting the seasoning into the chicken meat under the skin, coating as evenly as possible.

Place the drumsticks on the baking sheet and place into the oven for 30 minutes, rotating the drumsticks halfway through. For extra-crispy skin, broil for the last 3 to 5 minutes.

Coat each drumstick with 1 tablespoon (15 ml) of BBQ sauce to serve.

LOW-CARB BBQ SAUCE
You might have to try a few low-carb BBQ sauces before you find your favorite one. You can make your own BBQ sauce (page 169) at home or check out the health-food section at the grocery store. Look for sauces without added sugar and that use low glycemic sweeteners. A personal favorite is Ken Davis 2 Carb. It's sweetened with erythritol and comes in spicy and regular.

PER SERVING: 245 Calories, 5.4 g Total Carbs, 0.5 g Fiber, 2.9 g Net Carbs, 24.5 g Protein, 14.1 g Fat

STEAK BURRITO BOWL

Letting kids explore protein types is a great way to find out what they like. Chicken is easy and well liked, but you may be surprised to find that your little ones love steak too! This bowl is inspired by those delicious Mexican restaurant dishes but at a fraction of the cost. You may have a little room in your budget once you give up carbs, because you don't eat fast food as often. This is a good opportunity to try new foods or different qualities you may have not been able to budget for before.

Serves: 4

1½ lb (680 g) skirt steak

1 tsp chili powder

¼ tsp garlic powder

¼ tsp ground black pepper

1 tbsp (14 g) coconut oil

6 cups (282 g) chopped romaine lettuce

½ cup (120 g) mild salsa

1 cup (112 g) shredded Monterey Jack cheese

½ cup (120 g) Restaurant-Style Guacamole (page 178)

½ cup (120 g) sour cream

Sprinkle the steak with the chili powder, garlic powder and pepper. Melt the coconut oil in a skillet over medium-high heat and sear each side of the steak for about 3 minutes per side for medium rare. Use a meat thermometer and cook 1 to 2 minutes, or to your preferred doneness.

Let the steak rest for 10 minutes before slicing.

To assemble the bowls, place the romaine on the bottom. Add about 3 ounces (85 g) of steak per bowl. Top each bowl with 2 tablespoons (30 g) of salsa and ¼ cup (28 g) of cheese, 2 tablespoons (15 g) of guacamole and 2 tablespoons (15 g) of sour cream. Serve immediately.

SHORT ON TIME?

Grocery stores often carry shredded versions of heat-and-eat meats that are fully cooked and make this meal even quicker! Just be sure to check the label to avoid any carbs from sugary sauces. Shredded beef, chicken and pork are all tasty options!

PER SERVING: 681 Calories, 14.2 g Total Carbs, 4.8 g Fiber, 9.3 g Net Carbs, 55.8 g Protein, 45.3 g Fat

EVERYTHING BUT THE BUN CHEESEBURGER CASSEROLE

Casseroles can be a parent's best friend. This recipe utilizes all the classic cheeseburger toppings in one easy dish. Kids will love it because it tastes like the perfect bite of a cheeseburger, and parents will love it because it has a short prep time, leaving more time to relax with the family. Feel free to add your family's favorites, such as bacon or jalapeños or even top with shredded lettuce for a little crunch!

Serves: 4

1 lb (454 g) ground beef

¼ cup (40 g) chopped white onion

¼ tsp garlic powder

2 large eggs

1 (14.5-oz [411-g]) can diced tomatoes, drained

4 oz (113 g) softened cream cheese

1 cup (112 g) shredded mild cheddar cheese, divided

¼ cup (35 g) chopped dill pickles

¼ tsp sesame seeds

BBQ Sauce (page 169) or Burger Sauce (page 181), for serving

Preheat the oven to 375°F (190°C) and spray an 8 x 8-inch (20 x 20-cm) baking dish with nonstick cooking spray.

In a skillet over medium heat, brown the ground beef until it is fully cooked and no pink remains, about 7 to 10 minutes.

Carefully drain the grease from the pan and return the pan to the heat. Add the onions and garlic powder. Cook for 3 to 5 minutes, until the onions begin to soften.

Place the meat mixture in a large bowl and allow it to cool for 5 minutes. Crack the eggs into the bowl, add the diced tomatoes and stir into the meat mixture. Fold in the cream cheese and ½ cup (56 g) of the cheddar cheese.

Spoon the casserole into the baking dish. Top the casserole with the remaining ½ cup (56 g) of cheddar and place it into the oven. Bake for 20 to 25 minutes, or until the top is golden brown and the casserole is bubbling. Allow it to cool for 10 minutes before serving.

To serve, sprinkle the pickles and sesame seeds onto the casserole. Enjoy it with your favorite sauce, like BBQ (page 169), or try a tangy Burger Sauce (page 181).

PER SERVING: 631 Calories, 3.1 g Total Carbs, 0.1 g Fiber, 1.7 g Net Carbs, 28 g Protein, 56.1 g Fat

SUPER-STUFFED JUMBO CALZONES

I've simplified my most popular recipe for busy parents. These calzones are incredibly filling and so savory that you will be impressed they're Keto-friendly! The kids can help prep the ingredients and even customize their own calzone.

Serves: 6

1½ cups (170 g) shredded mozzarella cheese

¾ cup (84 g) blanched, finely ground almond flour

2 oz (56 g) cream cheese

1 large egg

½ tsp baking soda

½ cup (56 g) shredded mild cheddar cheese

14 slices (30 g) pepperoni, chopped

½ lb (224 g) cooked ground sausage

2 tbsp (10 g) grated Parmesan cheese

2 tbsp (30 ml) melted butter

½ tsp dried parsley

½ cup (120 ml) Mouthwatering Marinara (page 170)

Preheat the oven to 400°F (200°C).

Place the mozzarella cheese and almond flour in a microwave-safe bowl. Break the cream cheese into small pieces and add it to the bowl. Place the bowl in the microwave for 1 minute. Stir quickly until a ball forms, about 30 seconds. Add the egg and baking soda to the bowl and stir until fully combined. It may be easier to work the egg in with wet hands, folding the dough as you go. When it's complete, a smooth ball of dough will form.

Split the ball of dough into two pieces. Place one piece of dough in between two pieces of parchment and roll it into a circle until it is about ½ inch (1.3 cm) thick. Repeat with the second piece of dough.

Place each flattened round onto a parchment-lined baking sheet. On one half of each of the dough rounds, sprinkle the cheddar cheese, pepperoni and sausage, splitting the ingredients evenly between the two calzones.

To seal each calzone, carefully fold in half. Wet your fingers and pinch each closed, rolling up and pinching again to ensure it is fully closed. Bake the calzones for 20 to 25 minutes, or until golden brown.

In a small bowl, mix the Parmesan, butter and parsley. Brush it over the calzones. Allow them to cool for at least 10 minutes before serving.

Serve warm with a side of Mouthwatering Marinara (page 170) for dipping.

*See photo on page 60.

PER SERVING: 417 Calories, 6.7 g Total Carbs, 1.5 g Fiber, 5.2 g Net Carbs, 23.4 g Protein, 32.2 g Fat

KIDS, YOU CAN HELP!
You can help by sprinkling the toppings on the dough before baking. Make sure each calzone gets some cheese, pepperoni and sausage.

TACO TUESDAY EMPANADAS

Traditionally, empanadas are made with bleached wheat flour, which is high in carbs. For this recipe, I recommend blanched, finely ground almond flour, such as King Arthur or Bob's Red Mill. I would avoid almond meal, which is more coarsely ground and has a more prominent nut taste. The almond flour dough makes a delicious and crispy crust around a Mexican-inspired beef filling. Kids will love this recipe, because empanadas are portable for busy little ones on the go, and they can dip the empanadas in their favorite taco sauces!

Serves: 4

½ lb (226 g) ground beef

2 tbsp (30 ml) water

1 tsp chili powder

½ tsp ground cumin

¼ tsp garlic powder

¼ tsp oregano

1½ cups (170 g) shredded mozzarella cheese

¾ cup (84 g) blanched, finely ground almond flour

2 oz (56 g) cream cheese

1 egg

½ tsp baking soda

Preheat the oven to 400°F (200°C) and line a large baking sheet with parchment. Set aside.

To make the filling, brown the ground beef in a skillet over medium heat until no pink remains, about 7 to 10 minutes. Drain the grease from the beef and place the pan back onto the stovetop.

Pour the water into the pan with the meat and add the chili powder, cumin, garlic powder and oregano. Use a spatula to stir until the seasoning coats all of the meat. Cook for 3 to 5 minutes until the remaining water has evaporated.

Remove the pan from the heat and set it aside to cool.

To make the dough, place the mozzarella and almond flour into a large microwave-safe bowl. Break the cream cheese into small pieces, and then add it to the bowl. Place in the microwave for 1 minute.

Stir the melted cheese mixture together quickly with a fork or spoon until a ball forms. Add the egg and sprinkle the baking soda over the dough. Quickly stir to incorporate the egg, using wet hands to knead the dough if necessary. When the dough is ready, a smooth ball should form.

If the dough sits or becomes too cold, it will not be easy to use. If this happens, place it into the mixing bowl and reheat it in the microwave in 10-second increments.

(continued)

TACO TUESDAY EMPANADAS (CONTINUED)

½ cup (56 g) shredded mild cheddar cheese

½ cup (120 g) salsa, optional, for dipping

¼ cup (60 g) sour cream, optional, for dipping

¼ cup (60 g) Restaurant-Style Guacamole (page 178), optional, for dipping

Once the dough forms a ball, cut it into four sections. Place the dough pieces onto parchment paper and press out into ovals, about ¼ inch (6 mm) thick.

Divide the cooked meat into four sections and place one section onto half of each of the empanadas. Sprinkle each with 2 tablespoons (14 g) of cheddar.

Fold each empanada and press the edges to seal closed, rolling gently closed if needed.

Place the empanadas on the baking sheet and place into the oven. Bake for 25 minutes, or until the outside turns dark golden brown.

Remove the empanadas from the oven and allow them to cool for 10 minutes. For dipping, serve with salsa, sour cream and Restaurant-Style Guacamole (page 178), if desired.

PER SERVING: 615 Calories, 15.2 g Total Carbs, 4.7 g Fiber, 10.5 g Net Carbs, 31.7 g Protein, 47.9 g Fat

CHICKEN ENCHILADA BAKE

This is one of those meals you make in a hurry but ends up being one of your family's favorites! Green enchilada sauce is tangy and packed with flavor. It's made from tomatillos and green chilies, and paired with the sour cream this is a dish that can't be beat. To make this meal even faster, you can pick up a rotisserie chicken from the store, then debone and dice up the meat.

Serves: 4

½ cup (120 ml) green enchilada sauce

4 oz (112 g) softened cream cheese

¼ cup (60 g) sour cream

4 cups (500 g) cooked, diced chicken thigh

1½ cups (170 g) shredded Monterey Jack cheese

¼ cup (4 g) chopped fresh cilantro

1 avocado, diced

Preheat the oven to 375°F (190°C) and spray an 8 x 8–inch (20 x 20–cm) baking dish with nonstick cooking spray.

In a large bowl, mix the enchilada sauce, cream cheese and sour cream. Mix the chicken into the sauce and spoon the mixture into the baking dish.

Cover the mixture with the Monterey Jack cheese and place it into the oven for 25 minutes or until bubbling and the top begins to brown.

Sprinkle cilantro and avocado on top of the dish before serving.

PER SERVING: 680 Calories, 9.4 g Total Carbs, 3.2 g Fiber, 6.1 g Net Carbs, 29.1 g Protein, 60.7 g Fat

CHEESY CHICKEN SLIDERS

These sliders are easy to prepare and can be customized with your favorite flavors. Using ground chicken is a great alternative to beef because it complements many flavors, and you can more easily control the amount of fat in the meal. Healthy fat, such as mashed avocado, is a great option to top these and will keep your kids full until breakfast. If you love meal prep, these can also be frozen. Just be sure to separate the raw patties with parchment and keep them in a sealed freezer bag.

Yield: 6 sliders, 1 per serving

1 lb (454 g) ground chicken breast

¼ cup (40 g) diced yellow onion

¼ cup (45 g) diced green bell pepper

½ cup (56 g) shredded mozzarella cheese

¼ tsp salt

¼ tsp dried parsley

¼ tsp garlic powder

⅛ tsp ground black pepper

1 tbsp (14 g) coconut oil

Lettuce for lettuce wraps or Magical Keto Rolls (page 59), for serving

In a large bowl, mix the ground chicken with the onion and bell pepper. Fold in the mozzarella and add the salt, parsley, garlic powder and black pepper.

Form the meat into six balls and flatten them into patties. Heat your skillet over medium heat and melt the coconut oil in the pan. Carefully place the patties into the pan, working in batches if necessary.

Cook for 5 minutes per side or until the meat is completely cooked and the internal temperature is at least 165°F (75°C).

Enjoy on a lettuce wrap or a Magical Keto Roll (page 59).

MAKE IT YOUR OWN!
Bacon, avocado, grilled mushrooms and jalapeños are all great low-carb options for topping your burger! Give it a fun twist by adding taco seasoning to your mix and top with fresh pico de gallo.

PER SERVING: 175 Calories, 1.3 g Total Carbs, 0.2 g Fiber, 1.1 g Net Carbs, 26 g Protein, 7 g Fat

EASY TACO SOUP

Sometimes the best part of soup is all the fun things you can add as toppings. This soup comes together quickly but definitely isn't short on flavor. Make a weeknight a little extra exciting for the family by making a taco soup bar! Set out all their favorite taco fillings so everyone can load up their bowls. If you like a little crunch, check the deli section of your local grocery store for cheese crisps made with 100 percent cheese and crumble them on top of your soup!

Yield: 6 bowls, ¾ cup (180 ml) per serving

1 lb (454 g) 80/20 ground beef

1 tbsp (8 g) chili powder

2 tsp (4 g) ground cumin

¼ tsp garlic powder

1 tbsp (14 g) butter

¼ cup (40 g) chopped white onion

1 (10-oz [284-g]) can diced tomatoes with green chilies, drained

3 cups (720 ml) beef broth

¼ tsp xanthan gum

1 avocado, pitted, peeled and diced

1 Roma tomato, diced

1 cup (112 g) shredded mild cheddar cheese

¼ cup (60 g) sour cream

¼ cup (4 g) chopped fresh cilantro

In a large pot over medium heat, brown the ground beef until no pink remains, about 7 to 10 minutes. Drain the grease and add the chili powder, cumin and garlic powder to the pan. Stir to coat the meat.

Add the butter and onion to the pan, cooking until the onion begins to soften, about 2 to 3 minutes. Add the drained diced tomatoes and broth. Bring the soup to a boil for 5 minutes, then reduce the heat.

Add the xanthan gum and let the soup simmer for 15 minutes to allow it to thicken.

Separate into six bowls to serve. Top with avocado, Roma tomato, cheddar, sour cream and a sprinkle of cilantro for garnish.

PER SERVING: 670 Calories, 14 g Total Carbs, 5.2 g Fiber, 8.8 g Net Carbs, 27 g Protein, 56.4 g Fat

BROCCOLI-CHEDDAR SOUP

This soup is perfect for the kids and grown-ups too! It's not quite as thick as the broccoli-cheddar soup you may be used to, but that's because those soups use a roux made of flour and milk to make them thicker. If you prefer a thicker soup, you can add xanthan gum. It's a popular gluten-free powder that can be added to soups or sauces to thicken them. You can find the packets in the baking aisle for just a couple of dollars for three packets. The kids will love this soup because of its ultra-cheesy taste and delicious flavors. This soup pairs great with Magical Keto Rolls (page 59)!

Serves: 4

2 tbsp (28 g) butter

¼ cup (40 g) chopped yellow onion

½ tsp finely minced garlic

3 cups (720 ml) chicken broth

1 cup (90 g) chopped broccoli

2 oz (56 g) softened cream cheese

¼ cup (60 ml) heavy whipping cream

¼ tsp xanthan gum

1 cup (112 g) shredded sharp cheddar cheese

4 slices cooked, crumbled bacon

In a large pot over medium heat, melt the butter. Sauté the onion until it softens, about 3 minutes.

Add the garlic and sauté for 30 seconds, and then pour in the broth and broccoli. Bring the soup to a boil then reduce to a simmer for 10 minutes.

In a small bowl, whisk the cream cheese and heavy cream together. Pour it into the pot and stir.

Sprinkle in the xanthan gum and allow 3 to 5 minutes for the soup to thicken, stirring occasionally as needed.

Remove the pot from the heat and add in the shredded cheddar. Whisk quickly to fully melt the cheese and prevent sticking. Sprinkle the bacon over the top. Serve warm.

PER SERVING: 302 Calories, 5.1 g Total Carbs, 0.8 g Fiber, 4.3 g Net Carbs, 11.7 g Protein, 25.6 g Fat

CHICKEN ZOODLE SOUP

When the little ones aren't feeling well, sometimes a nice warm soup is just what they need. Traditionally, this soup has noodles made of flour, and while the kids may enjoy those, they don't add a lot of extra vitamins. This recipe opts for lower carb zucchini noodles, which contain a dose of vitamin C to help your family kick the colds. Feel free to add extra low-carb veggies if you prefer a bulkier soup. Spinach can be a great addition and is full of nutrients.

Serves: 4

2 tbsp (28 g) butter

¼ cup (40 g) chopped onion

2 celery ribs, chopped

1 clove garlic, finely minced

4 cups (960 ml) chicken broth

1 bay leaf

1 tsp dried parsley

¼ tsp ground black pepper

½ tsp pink salt

¼ tsp dried thyme

2 cups (280 g) cooked, cubed chicken

2 medium zucchinis, spiralized

In a large pot over medium heat, melt the butter. Add the onion and celery. Sauté for 2 to 3 minutes, or until the onion softens and becomes fragrant. Add the garlic and cook for 30 seconds.

Pour the broth into the pot and add the bay leaf, parsley, pepper, salt and thyme and stir. Add the chicken and bring the pot to a boil for 2 minutes, then lower the heat and simmer for 10 minutes.

After 10 minutes, add the zucchinis and turn off the heat. Stir occasionally and let the zucchinis soften for 5 to 7 minutes. They should be soft but still firm enough to add a bit of texture to the dish. Discard the bay leaf before serving.

DON'T HAVE A SPIRALIZER?

If you don't have a spiralizer, you can also use a cheese grater to slice the zucchini into ribbons or shreds. The cook time won't change, and you'll still have a nutritious, filling meal in just minutes.

PER SERVING: 200 Calories, 6.2 g Total Carbs, 1.7 g Fiber, 4.5 g Net Carbs, 24.1 g Protein, 8.3 g Fat

SWIMMING SALMON PATTIES

Salmon not only has protein and healthy fats, it's also loaded with omega-3s, which are important for growth and development in children. This recipe is great both for those kids who are new to seafood and for those who already love it. The patties form a golden crust, and they have a crunch that is undeniably good, even to the pickiest of eaters.

Yield: 6 patties, 1 per serving

2 (5-oz [284-g]) pouches pink salmon

1 large egg

2 tbsp (26 g) mayo

¼ tsp garlic powder

¼ tsp chili powder

½ oz (14 g) plain, finely ground pork rinds

2 tbsp (28 g) coconut oil, for frying

Place a paper towel on a large, flat dish or dinner plate.

In a large bowl, mix the salmon, egg, mayo, garlic powder, chili powder and pork rinds until fully combined.

Form the mixture into six small patties. Melt the coconut oil in a skillet over medium heat. Fry the patties for 4 to 5 minutes per side, or until each side is golden and crispy.

Place the patties on the paper towel–lined dish to absorb the excess oil and let them cool for at least 5 minutes before serving.

MAKE IT TODDLER-FRIENDLY!
To make this meal toddler-friendly, let the patties completely cool and break them into smaller pieces. Serve with mashed avocado for an added boost of nutrients and healthy fats. This is one of my daughter's favorites!

PER SERVING: 120 Calories, 0.4 g Total Carbs, 0.05 g Fiber, 0.4 g Net Carbs, 7.4 g Protein, 9.9 g Fat

SNEAKY SPAGHETTI SQUASH LASAGNA

When cooking for kids, you have to think ahead to taste, texture, smell and appearance. This is why I love spaghetti squash. It looks very similar to angel hair pasta and has a sweet but mild taste that kids don't seem to mind, especially when covered in meat and cheese.

Serves: 6

1 (4-lb [1.8-kg]) spaghetti squash

1 lb (454 g) 80/20 ground beef

½ cup (113 g) Mouthwatering Marinara (page 170)

Salt, to taste

1 cup (246 g) ricotta cheese

¼ cup (15 g) grated Parmesan cheese

¼ tsp dried oregano

¼ tsp dried basil

¼ tsp ground black pepper

1 cup (112 g) shredded mozzarella cheese, divided

Preheat the oven to 350°F (180°C). Spray nonstick cooking spray into an 8 x 8-inch (20 x 20-cm) baking dish.

Cut the spaghetti squash in half and scoop out the seeds. Place it cut side down into a microwave-safe baking dish. Pour in enough water to fill about 1 inch (2.5 cm) of the dish. Microwave for 10 to 12 minutes, or until you can easily pierce the squash with a fork. Microwaves vary in wattage, so you may need to reduce or increase the time to get it just right.

In a skillet over medium heat, cook the ground beef until no pink remains, about 7 to 10 minutes. Drain the grease from the pan and return it to the heat. Pour the marinara into the pan with the beef and reduce the heat. Let it simmer for 10 minutes. Add salt to taste.

In a small bowl, mix the ricotta, Parmesan, oregano, basil and pepper. Set aside.

Use a fork to pull apart the squash strands and place them into a bowl.

Place one-fourth of the beef mixture on the bottom of the baking dish. Place one-fourth of the squash strands on top of the sauce. Spoon one-fourth of the ricotta mixture on top of the squash. Top with one-fourth of the mozzarella. Repeat the layering three times until all the ingredients have been used. Bake for 20 minutes until bubbling and browned. Let cool for 10 minutes before serving. Serve warm.

PER SERVING: 432 Calories, 8.6 g Total Carbs, 1.3 g Fiber, 7.3 g Net Carbs, 23.3 g Protein, 34.5 g Fat

KIDS, YOU CAN HELP!
When the squash is cooked and cooled, use a fork to pull the spaghetti pieces out. You'll be amazed by how much spaghetti you can get! Race your grown-ups to see who can get the most out of their half.

SMALL BITES WITH BIG FLAVOR

KIDS MIGHT BE SMALL, BUT THEY SURE ARE POWERFUL—just like each and every dish in this chapter! These fast, Keto-friendly foods, packed with flavor and nutrition, make the perfect snack for after school, before bedtime or any time you don't need a full meal.

In the upcoming pages, you'll see everything from Poppable Pumpkin Muffins (page 88) to Pigs in a Blanket (page 95)—all made to low-carb perfection! The best part is, these recipes don't skimp on flavor one bit. They are just what you need to help you power through your day.

Get ready to share (or keep them to yourself . . . I won't tell!) some of the most delicious, healthy snacks you've ever made. You'll soon realize these small bites are just as awesome as you are!

POPPABLE PUMPKIN MUFFINS

Mini muffins are a great snack for kids, but often you'll find the prepackaged ones are loaded with unnecessary added sugar. A popular brand in the stores has 16 grams of added sugar. That's about 4 teaspoons in one small package! These muffins embrace the natural sweetness of pumpkin to make a much more nutritious snack.

Yield: 20 muffins, 2 per serving

1¼ cups (140 g) blanched, finely ground almond flour

¼ cup (50 g) granular erythritol

2 tsp (8 g) baking powder

2 eggs

3 tbsp (45 ml) melted butter

¼ cup (61 g) pure pumpkin puree

¼ tsp cinnamon

½ tsp pumpkin spice

½ tsp vanilla extract

Preheat the oven to 350°F (180°C) and prepare a mini muffin tin.

In a large bowl, whisk together the almond flour, erythritol and baking powder. Add the eggs to the bowl and whisk.

While mixing, pour in the butter, pumpkin puree, cinnamon, pumpkin spice and vanilla. Continue stirring until few lumps remain.

Spoon about 1 tablespoon (15 g) into each well of the muffin tin. Bake the muffins for 10 to 12 minutes, or until the tops begin to turn light brown. Let them cool for at least 30 minutes before removing from the tin to avoid crumbling.

Store leftovers in a sealed freezer bag or airtight container in the fridge for up to 4 days for the best flavor.

MAKE IT YOUR OWN!
If you don't like pumpkin or don't have any on hand, no problem! Replace the puree in this recipe with ¼ cup (60 ml) of unsweetened almond milk. You can add blackberries for a tart twist or 1 tablespoon (15 ml) of banana extract and ¼ cup (30 g) of finely chopped walnuts for a "faux" banana-nut muffin.

PER SERVING: 125 Calories, 10.3 g Total Carbs, 1.7 g Fiber, 4.8 g Sugar Alcohols, 3.8 g Net Carbs, 4.8 g Protein, 9.3 g Fat

COOKIE DOUGH BITES

These eggless cookie dough bites are the perfect weekend treat! They're creamy and have all the flavors you love in cookie dough. These are meant to be enjoyed in moderation because they're higher in calories, so you don't need much to keep you full. Try using your favorite cookie add-ins like chopped nuts or a little nut butter to change things up! This recipe is so simple the kids can even make it on their own! It's a great way to practice counting, measuring and building their confidence in the kitchen!

Yield: 12 bites, 1 per serving

8 oz (224 g) softened cream cheese

4 tbsp (56 g) softened butter

½ cup (60 g) powdered erythritol

1 tsp vanilla extract

¼ cup (28 g) blanched, finely ground almond flour

¼ cup (45 g) low-carb chocolate chips

In a large bowl, mix the cream cheese, butter and erythritol until smooth. Add the vanilla and almond flour. Fold in the chocolate chips.

Use a 2-tablespoon (30-g) cookie dough scoop to make 12 bites. Place each scoop of dough into a mini muffin liner and put them all on a plate. Cover and refrigerate for at least 2 hours. Serve chilled.

LOW-CARB CHOCOLATE CHIPS

There are lots of sugar-free chocolate chips on the market, but not all are the best choice for Ketogenic or low-carb diets. Oftentimes, companies will use maltitol, a sugar replacement, that has a high blood-glucose impact. For a low-carb-friendly option in the health food section, look for those that are sweetened with Stevia, monk fruit or erythritol. These sugar replacements are low carb but also generally do not impact your blood sugar.

PER SERVING: 120 Calories, 9 g Total Carbs, 0.9 g Fiber, 6.5 g Sugar Alcohols, 1.7 g Net Carbs, 1.8 g Protein, 11.9 g Fat

ALMOND BUTTER COOKIE BALLS

These cookie balls are full of creamy almond butter and chocolate chips—and to top it off, they won't cause a sugar rush! They're made with no-sugar-added ingredients, which makes them low-carb, healthy bites. The added protein makes these an excellent snack for an energy boost or simply a dessert you can feel great eating any time of the day.

Yield: 20 cookie balls, 1 per serving

1 cup (250 g) no-added-sugar almond butter

¼ cup (48 g) low-carb protein powder

¼ cup (50 g) granular erythritol

¼ tsp cinnamon

½ tsp vanilla extract

1 egg

¼ cup (25 g) shredded, unsweetened coconut

¼ cup (45 g) low-carb chocolate chips

Preheat the oven to 350°F (175°C). Line a baking sheet with parchment.

Place the almond butter in a large mixing bowl. Add the protein powder, erythritol, cinnamon and vanilla to the bowl and use a large silicon spatula to mix them.

Crack open the egg and stir it into the mixture.

Fold in the shredded coconut and chocolate chips. Form the dough into 2-inch (5-cm) balls and place them on the baking sheet.

Bake for 12 minutes. Allow the cookie balls to firm up and cool for at least 20 minutes before removing from the baking sheet.

PER SERVING: 96 Calories, 6.8 g Total Carbs, 2.2 g Fiber, 3.3 g Sugar Alcohols, 1.2 g Net Carbs, 4.3 g Protein, 8.1 g Fat

PIGS IN A BLANKET

This Keto spin on a classic favorite is just as tasty and even more cheesy than traditional pigs in a blanket! Kids will love dipping these into their favorite mustard or no-sugar-added ketchup. Beef hot dogs are a good option for this recipe. The brand Nathan's is a personal favorite because of the flavor and lack of casing, which makes them a bit easier for the kids to eat. They also don't have any nitrates or nitrites. Remember to read labels and choose a brand that's best for your family and budget.

Serves: 4

1 cup (112 g) shredded mozzarella cheese

½ cup (56 g) blanched, finely ground almond flour

1 oz (28 g) cream cheese

½ tsp baking soda

1 egg yolk

4 beef hot dogs

½ tsp sesame seeds

Mustard or Classic Ketchup (page 166), for dipping

Preheat the oven to 400°F (200°C) and line a medium-sized baking sheet with parchment.

In a large microwave-safe bowl, add the mozzarella and almond flour. Break the cream cheese into small pieces and add to the bowl. Microwave for 30 to 45 seconds, or until the cheese is melted.

Stir the mixture with a fork until a soft ball of dough forms. Sprinkle the dough with the baking soda and add the egg yolk. Break the yolk with a fork and stir it into the dough until a smooth ball forms.

Lay a piece of parchment paper on a flat work surface. Wet your hands with a bit of water and flatten out the dough to about 3 x 4 inches (7.5 x 10 cm) and about ½ inch (1.3 cm) thick.

Use a knife to cut the dough into four even pieces. Pat the hot dogs with a paper towel to remove surface moisture and gently wrap a piece of dough around each, leaving the ends exposed, pinching at the seam to close. The dough will expand a bit during baking, so try to wrap each as closely as possible without breaking the dough.

Place all the wrapped hot dogs on the baking sheet and sprinkle with sesame seeds. Bake for 20 minutes. The dough will turn golden and firmer when cooked. Remove from the oven and allow to cool for at least 10 minutes; otherwise, the dough may fall apart.

Serve with your favorite dipping sauces, such as mustard or Classic Ketchup (page 166).

PER SERVING: 333 Calories, 6.8 g Total Carbs, 1.6 g Fiber, 5.2 g Net Carbs, 17.5 g Protein, 25.8 g Fat

BACON-WRAPPED CHICKEN BITES

This protein-filled snack is great for those days when the kids' appetites seem bottomless. These can also be prepped at the beginning of the week and reheated to enjoy when hunger strikes throughout the week. If you don't like BBQ sauce, simply brush with a little mayo to keep the chicken moist and flavorful before wrapping in bacon.

Yield: 12 bites, 3 per serving

2 (6-oz [170-g]) boneless, skinless chicken breasts

¼ tsp garlic powder

¼ tsp ground black pepper

¼ cup (68 g) BBQ Sauce (page 169)

12 slices bacon

¼ cup (60 ml) Rockin' Ranch Dip (page 174), for dipping

Preheat the oven to 350°F (180°C). Line a baking sheet with foil, and then place a baking rack on top of the foil.

Cut the chicken into 2-inch (5-cm) cubes. Sprinkle the garlic powder and pepper onto the chicken. Pour the BBQ Sauce over the chicken and toss to coat.

Cut the bacon in half widthwise, and wrap each piece of chicken in bacon, securing it with a toothpick.

Place the bites onto the wire rack and bake for 35 to 40 minutes, or until the bacon is crispy and the chicken is fully cooked through to at least 165°F (75°C) internally.

Serve with ranch for dipping.

PER SERVING: 303 Calories, 5.7 g Total Carbs, 0.4 g Fiber, 3.4 g Net Carbs, 29.2 g Protein, 18.3 g Fat

CHEESY CAULIFLOWER SMILES

This recipe is inspired by potato smiles but with way fewer carbs and more nutrients! This recipe uses cauliflower and almond flour to make a dough that can be shaped like a happy, smiling face. Your little ones will be smiling back at them, and you'll be happy knowing they're eating food to fuel their bodies. If you're short on time, just roll these into tots!

Yield: 16 smiles, 2 per serving

½ cup (120 ml) water

1 medium head cauliflower

4 tbsp (28 g) blanched, finely ground almond flour

1 oz (28 g) cream cheese

½ cup (56 g) shredded sharp cheddar cheese

½ cup (40 g) grated Parmesan cheese

¼ tsp xanthan gum

Preheat the oven to 400°F (205°C).

Line a large baking sheet with parchment paper.

Place a steamer basket in a medium pot. Pour the water into the pot and bring to a boil. Remove the stems and leaves from the cauliflower, and then cut it into florets. Place them into the pot and cover for 15 minutes to steam until the cauliflower is tender.

Let the cauliflower cool and use a cheesecloth or clean towel to remove the excess moisture. Place the cauliflower in a food processor and add the almond flour, cream cheese, cheddar, Parmesan and xanthan gum. Process for 1 minute or until the dough is smooth. It will be sticky, but you will be able to roll it into balls.

Wet your hands, and then roll the mixture into sixteen balls on the parchment-lined sheet, about 2 tablespoons (30 g) each. Press each into a flat circle, about ¼ inch (6 mm) thick. Use a straw to poke two eyes into each round, and use a spoon to make a smile.

Bake for 12 to 15 minutes, or until golden brown. Serve warm.

PER SERVING: 208 Calories, 11.8 g Total Carbs, 3.7 g Fiber, 8.1 g Net Carbs, 11.9 g Protein, 13.5 g Fat

BACON, LETTUCE AND TOMATO DIP

If you love bacon, lettuce and tomatoes, this dip is for you. This is a recipe that's great for having the kids' help. Lots of mixing and no baking required! It's perfect to enjoy as a side with sandwiches, or as a snack or even a light meal. Pork rinds and low-carb veggie sticks, such as cucumbers and celery, make great dippers. This is a great dish to bring to the family picnic. Everyone will be amazed you get to eat this food all the time and still meet all the health goals for your family.

Serves: 8 (¼ cup [60 g] dip per serving)

8 oz (224 g) softened cream cheese

¼ cup (58 g) mayo

¼ cup (60 g) sour cream

1 cup (112 g) shredded mild cheddar cheese

1 cup (47 g) shredded romaine lettuce

2 Roma tomatoes, diced

8 slices cooked, crumbled, sugar-free bacon

Pork rinds, cucumbers and celery, for dipping

Set out an 8 x 8-inch (20 x 20-cm) serving dish or bowl.

In a large bowl, beat the cream cheese, mayo and sour cream until fluffy. Spoon the mixture into the bottom of the dish.

Sprinkle the cheddar, lettuce, tomatoes and bacon onto the cream cheese mixture. Serve with pork rinds and veggies for dipping.

PER SERVING: 268 Calories, 3.8 g Total Carbs, 0.5 g Fiber, 3.3 g Net Carbs, 8.8 g Protein, 24.7 g Fat

LOADED BROCCOLI

Broccoli on its own can be pretty boring, but it has so many healthy vitamins and nutrients, and something had to be done to make it more exciting to eat. Kids will love this dish because of the delicious cheese and bacon in every bite! My kids absolutely love the tang of sour cream too, which makes this dish reminiscent of a loaded baked potato. If you have a little extra time, you can also swap out the shredded cheese for a serving of ooey, gooey Cheese Sauce (page 173)!

Serves: 4

2 tbsp (28 g) coconut oil

4 cups (340 g) fresh broccoli florets

¼ cup (60 ml) water

½ tsp pink salt

2 tbsp (30 ml) melted butter

1 cup (112 g) shredded sharp cheddar cheese

8 tbsp (120 g) sour cream

8 slices cooked, crumbled bacon

In a large skillet over medium heat, warm the coconut oil. Add the broccoli and water to the pan and sprinkle with salt. Sauté for 7 to 10 minutes or until the broccoli is tender. Add a few tablespoons of water if needed.

Before removing from the pan, add the butter and toss the broccoli. To serve, place in bowls or a serving platter and top with cheddar, sour cream and crumbled bacon.

PER SERVING: 394 Calories, 7.4 g Total Carbs, 2.4 g Fiber, 5 g Net Carbs, 16.2 g Protein, 34.2 g Fat

AVOCADO TUNA SALAD

Whether your kiddo loves avocado or is a little reluctant to try it, this is a great recipe to introduce something new! Sometimes the key to getting them to try a new food is offering something familiar that incorporates the new food. My son doesn't like avocado, but I can usually get away with adding some to his beloved tuna salad without him noticing. The creaminess of the avocado blends right in and makes this meal even more nutrient packed.

Serves: 2

1 avocado

2 tbsp (26 g) mayo

½ tsp chili powder

Juice of ½ lime

2 celery ribs, diced

1 (11-oz [312-g]) pouch chunk light tuna in water

2 tbsp (2 g) chopped cilantro

8 leaves Bibb lettuce, for serving

In a large bowl, mash the avocado and mayo until mostly smooth. Sprinkle in the chili powder and lime juice.

Add the celery, tuna and cilantro and fold into the mashed avocado. Serve immediately on lettuce leaves.

KIDS, YOU CAN HELP!

Make a veggie platter to serve with this recipe. Ask your grown-up to slice up some veggies, such as cucumbers, red bell peppers, celery and broccoli. Then create a colorful display for all your family to enjoy!

PER SERVING: 224 Calories, 5.9 g Total Carbs, 3.9 g Fiber, 2 g Net Carbs, 20.9 g Protein, 13.3 g Fat

SUPER SIMPLE SEED CRACKERS

Flax crackers in the store can be a little expensive, close to $10 for a few servings, but luckily, they're super easy to make at home! You can find whole flaxseed in the baking aisle and often in the bulk section of your local health food market. These crackers are a unique alternative to carb-heavy crackers and offer lots of fiber, which is sure to keep your little ones' tummies happy!

Yield: 20 crackers, 5 per serving

1 cup (165 g) whole flaxseed

½ cup (120 ml) water

¼ tsp pink Himalayan salt

¼ tsp garlic powder

¼ tsp onion powder

In a large bowl, stir together the flaxseed, water, salt, garlic powder and onion powder. Cover with plastic and allow to sit for 30 minutes or until all the liquid has been soaked up. The flax will absorb most of the liquid and create a gelatinous-type texture.

Meanwhile, preheat the oven to 325°F (160°C) and line a large baking sheet with parchment.

Spread the flax mixture into a large rectangle, about ¼ inch (6 mm) thick.

Bake for 20 minutes, or until the center is no longer soft. Let it cool completely and roughly break into 2 x 2–inch (5 x 5–cm) squares. Store in a sealed freezer bag for up to 3 days.

TOP IT!

My personal favorite way to enjoy flax crackers is with a little bit of cream cheese and a couple slices of pepperoni. You can use these for dips, crumbled in salads or topped with your favorite meat and cheese combo, like turkey and cheddar, for a healthy and filling snack.

PER SERVING: 225 Calories, 12.5 g Total Carbs, 11.5 g Fiber, 1 g Net Carbs, 7.8 g Protein, 17.8 g Fat

ALMOND BUTTER FLAVOR BOMB

If the kiddos are feeling extra hungry, they might need a bit of extra fat to help satiate them. These flavor bombs are a special treat loaded with fat to help curb hunger. With just a few ingredients, these are easy to make and will remind you of candy treats. You can make them ahead of time and store them in the fridge or freezer. To make this recipe even more fun, find a cute silicone mold that the kids will love!

Yield: 8 mini bites

½ cup (112 g) refined coconut oil

½ cup (120 g) almond butter

2 tbsp (10 g) cacao powder

2 tbsp (15 g) powdered erythritol

In a large microwave-safe bowl, melt the coconut oil and almond butter. Stir in the cacao powder and erythritol.

Place 10 mini muffin tin liners into a tin. Scoop 2 tablespoons (30 g) of the mixture into each liner. Cover and place into the freezer for 30 minutes to harden.

Remove the flavor bombs with their liners from the tin and place them into a sealed freezer bag. Store in the fridge for up to 1 week.

Serve chilled; these melt quickly.

PER SERVING: 230 Calories, 6.75 g Total Carbs, 2.5 g Fiber, 3 g Sugar Alcohols, 1.25 g Net Carbs, 3.75 g Protein, 22.5 g Fat

SUNSHINE GUMMIES

Gummies are so easy to make at home and come at a fraction of the cost of the sugary ones you can buy in the store. These use lemon juice for a little tang, but you can also add a sprinkle of citric acid to make them sour. You can find citric acid near the jars and canning section of the store. You can also make these with your favorite water enhancer, like Mio. Just add a few squirts to taste and omit the erythritol.

Yield: 8 servings, 9 (1-inch [2.5-cm]) gummies per serving

1¼ cups (300 ml) water

4 tbsp (28 g) unflavored gelatin

1 tbsp (14 g) coconut oil

2 tbsp (15 g) powdered erythritol

½ cup (120 ml) lemon juice

In a saucepan over medium heat, bring the water to a boil. Stir in the gelatin until no lumps remain. Turn off the heat and add the coconut oil, erythritol and lemon juice.

Use a dropper or teaspoon to fill 1-inch (2.5-cm) silicone molds. Place the mold on a cutting board and cover. Place into the freezer for 30 minutes, or until firm. Remove the gummies from molds and store in a sealed freezer bag in the fridge for up to 4 days.

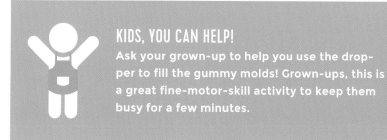

KIDS, YOU CAN HELP!
Ask your grown-up to help you use the dropper to fill the gummy molds! Grown-ups, this is a great fine-motor-skill activity to keep them busy for a few minutes.

PER SERVING: 33 Calories, 4 g Total Carbs, 0 g Fiber, 3 g Sugar Alcohols, 1 g Net Carbs, 3.5 g Protein, 1.7 g Fat

KICKIN' CHICKEN CHEESE STICKS

These are some of the easiest cheese sticks I've ever made. No dealing with dough, just a quick mix in the bowl and baking. If your kids like pizza cheese sticks, the kind that look like cheese pizza cut into strips, this will become a favorite of theirs! Don't be afraid of adding the buffalo sauce. The amount is just enough for flavor without being spicy for the little ones. This base is so customizable, you'll find yourself making it all the time. Feel free to leave out the chicken and add your favorite protein. I love customizing these with crumbled bacon or even just making them with cheese and dipping in low-carb marinara sauce.

Serves: 4

1 cup (112 g) shredded mozzarella cheese

1 large egg

1 cup (125 g) cooked, shredded chicken

¼ cup (60 ml) buffalo sauce

Mouthwatering Marinara (page 170) or Rockin' Ranch Dip (page 174), for serving

Preheat the oven to 350°F (180°C) and line a large baking sheet with parchment.

In a large bowl, mix the cheese and egg.

In a medium bowl, mix the chicken and buffalo sauce and then fold it into the cheese mixture.

Scoop the chicken mixture onto the parchment paper. Wet your hands with a bit of water and press the mixture into a circle about ½ inch (1.3 cm) thick.

Place the baking sheet in the oven and bake for 20 minutes or until it's bubbling and beginning to brown.

Let it cool for at least 10 minutes before cutting into strips. Serve with low-carb marinara or ranch.

PER SERVING: 127 Calories, 1 g Total Carbs, 0 g Fiber, 1 g Net Carbs, 14.6 g Protein, 6.6 g Fat

LOW-CARB MARINARA

If you don't have time to make your own Mouthwatering Marinara (page 170), there are some good store-bought options out there; you just have to be sure to check the label. Try looking in the health food section of the store. Look for sauces that don't have added sugar or sweetener and keep the carbs below 5 grams. Tomatoes naturally have carbs, so you're likely to see carbs on the label, but you'll know if there's added sugar. A personal favorite is Rao's Marinara.

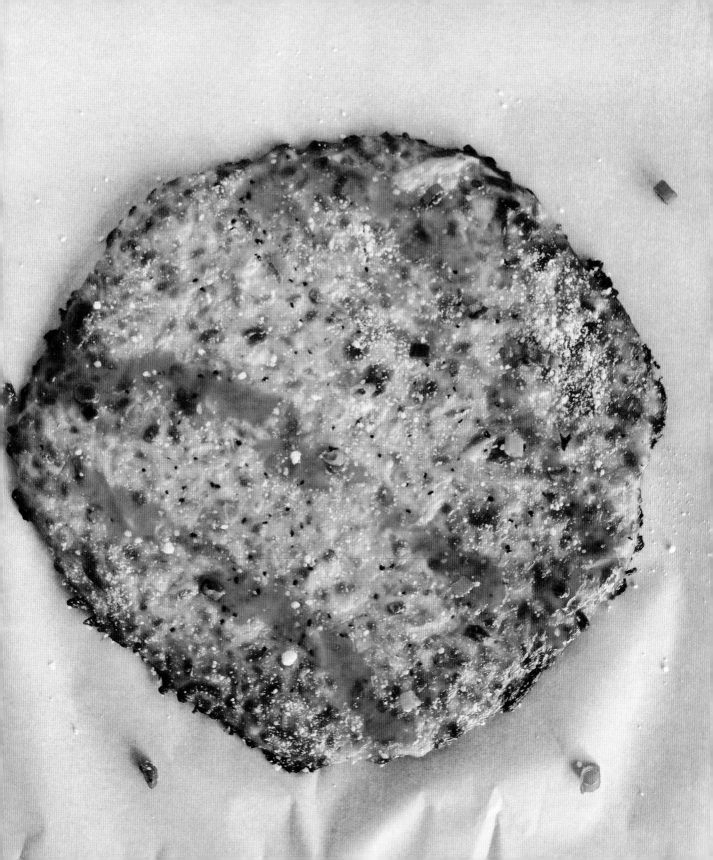

CHEESY GARLIC DROP BISCUITS

If you're in need of a quick side dish, look no further! These biscuits come together easily and add extra flavor to any meal. By using only a spoon to drop these onto the sheet, rather than rolling them, they stay airy and have lots of extra crunchy spots on top where they get extra golden brown. You can also split the leftover biscuits and use them as mini sandwich buns for the kiddos.

Serves: 8

1½ cups (168 g) blanched, finely ground almond flour

2 tsp (8 g) baking powder

1 egg

3 tbsp (42 g) softened butter

¼ tsp garlic powder

½ cup (56 g) shredded sharp cheddar cheese

Preheat the oven to 350°F (180°C). Line a baking sheet with parchment.

In a large bowl, mix the almond flour and baking powder. Add in the egg, butter, garlic powder and cheddar and continue stirring until fully combined. A soft and light dough should form.

Use a serving spoon to take a scoop of the mixture and drop it onto the baking sheet, one scoop at a time, making eight biscuits.

Bake for 12 to 14 minutes or until the biscuits begin to turn brown around the edges.

Let the biscuits cool for at least 15 minutes before serving.

KIDS, YOU CAN HELP!
This recipe needs strong arms to stir! Help your grown-up make yummy, cheesy biscuits by being the designated stirrer. Be sure to listen closely to the grown-up for directions, and stir slowly so the ingredients don't try to jump out of the bowl!

PER SERVING: 189 Calories, 7.3 g Total Carbs, 2.3 g Fiber, 5 g Net Carbs, 7.8 g Protein, 14.6 g Fat

RISE AND SHINE BREAKFASTS

BREAKFAST CONTINUES TO BE THE MOST IMPORTANT MEAL OF THE DAY for your Keto diet. The food you choose to start your day with can help decide how full, focused and energized you are throughout the rest of your day.

You might be worried that not all of your family's favorite breakfast foods fit into your low-carb lifestyle, but the good news is, not only do they fit, they're also just as delicious! It just takes a little extra creativity in the kitchen.

With everything from French Toast Sticks (page 119) to a Make-Ahead Breakfast Sandwich (page 136), your new breakfast routine is going to make you want to jump out of bed in the morning, so you don't miss a single bite!

FRENCH TOAST STICKS

French Toast Sticks are a yummy, handheld way to enjoy a quick breakfast, especially when you dunk them in sugar-free syrup, dust them with powdered sweetener . . . or both! For this recipe, you'll be baking a sweet custard loaf that can be enjoyed just like French toast. These have the classic eggy taste of French toast but without the bread—I promise you won't even miss it!

Yield: 20 slices, 2 per serving

8 large eggs

1 tsp vanilla extract

½ cup (60 ml) heavy whipping cream

½ cup (56 g) blanched, finely ground almond flour

¼ cup (50 g) granular erythritol

¼ tsp cinnamon

½ tsp baking powder

2 tsp (9 g) butter

KETO-FRIENDLY SYRUP

A lot of sugar-free syrups have a tricky ingredient called maltitol. This makes them taste just like the sugary original, but it causes tummy troubles. Choc Zero is a great alternative available online. Only 1 gram of net carbs per serving! You can also add a couple drops of maple extract to the melted butter for a quick alternative.

Preheat the oven to 350°F (180°C) and spray a 9 x 5-inch (23 x 13-cm) loaf pan with a nonstick spray.

Crack the eggs into a large bowl. Whisk together with the vanilla and heavy whipping cream until smooth.

In a medium mixing bowl, whisk together the almond flour, erythritol, cinnamon and baking powder. Slowly stir the dry ingredients into the egg mixture in the large bowl. Continue gently stirring until all the ingredients form a smooth, pourable batter.

Pour the batter into the loaf pan and bake for 30 minutes.

When completely cooked, the loaf will be golden on the top and puffed up. It will sink down into the pan as it cools and form a dense loaf.

Allow the loaf to cool completely, or, if possible, at least 30 to 45 minutes before slicing. If it's sliced when it's hot, the pieces may crumble.

Slice the loaf into twenty pieces. In a skillet over medium heat, melt the butter. When the pan is hot, add your desired amount of French toast sticks to the pan to toast until golden on each side, about 3 to 5 minutes.

Depending on your personal preference, you may want to toast all the sticks at once and store in an airtight container in the fridge up to 4 days, microwaving for 30 seconds to heat. Alternatively, you may place the untoasted slices in an airtight container in the fridge and warm in the skillet with butter or coconut oil.

PER SERVING: 154 Calories, 7.6 g Total Carbs, 0.6 g Fiber, 4.8 g Sugar Alcohols, 2.1 g Net Carbs, 6.4 g Protein, 12.6 g Fat

PIZZA BAKED EGGS

Who said you can't have pizza for breakfast? This recipe—a fun twist on boring eggs—will start your day right by filling you up with all the savory flavor you can expect from your favorite pizza toppings! Let the kids help by setting out some ingredient options, even chopped veggies, and let them build their own. You might be surprised with what they choose!

Serves: 4

4 tsp (19 g) butter

8 eggs

20 slices pepperoni

1 cup (112 g) mozzarella cheese

¼ cup (20 g) grated Parmesan cheese

¼ tsp garlic powder

¼ tsp oregano

Preheat the oven to 375°F (190°C). Prepare four (4-inch [10-cm]) ramekins by greasing each one with a teaspoon of butter. Set out a medium baking sheet. Crack the eggs, two into each ramekin.

Slice the pepperoni into strips and evenly distribute among each ramekin, placing them on top of the eggs. Sprinkle each ramekin with mozzarella and Parmesan. Top each with garlic powder and oregano.

Place the ramekins on the baking sheet and bake for 15 minutes. Serve warm.

KIDS, YOU CAN HELP!
You can add the fun toppings. Sprinkle each dish with your favorite veggies, meat and cheese to create a breakfast masterpiece!

PER SERVING: 299 Calories, 2.9 g Total Carbs, 0.3 g Fiber, 2.6 g Net Carbs, 17 g Protein, 20 g Fat

CHOCOLATE-DIPPED STRAWBERRY CREPES

Sometimes all you need to get kids excited about their food is a creative presentation. While this recipe can also make great thin pancakes, turning those pancakes into crepes and stuffing them with berries and whipped cream really takes the experience up a notch. Feel free to change things up by using your favorite no-sugar-added fruit preserves or even no-sugar-added natural peanut butter for a PB & J–style crepe.

Serves: 4

4 oz (112 g) softened cream cheese

4 eggs

2 tbsp (15 g) powdered erythritol

½ tsp vanilla extract

1 tsp coconut oil

1 cup (240 g) sugar-free Whipped Cream (page 124)

8 medium strawberries, sliced

2 oz (60 ml) melted, sugar-free, low-carb chocolate

Place the cream cheese, eggs, erythritol and vanilla into a blender. Blend until a smooth, thin batter forms, scraping down the sides as needed.

In a medium nonstick skillet over medium heat, melt the coconut oil and pour in a quarter of the batter while tilting the pan so the batter covers the bottom. Allow to cook for 2 to 4 minutes until golden brown, and then carefully flip and cook for 30 to 45 seconds.

Place finished crepes on a plate to cool.

To serve, place ¼ cup (60 g) of the whipped cream onto half of each crepe, add two sliced strawberries and fold the crepe in half, then in half again, to form a triangle. Drizzle with chocolate and serve warm.

KETO-FRIENDLY CHOCOLATE
While chocolate naturally has a little sugar in it, it is possible to find chocolate bars that don't have excessive added sugars. A personal favorite is Lily's Chocolate, which comes in multiple flavors and is often found in the health food section of grocery stores. Look for chocolate bars sweetened with Stevia or erythritol. Many brands that make regular, full-sugar chocolate bars make "sugar-free" bars that are sweetened with maltitol, which is known for causing tummy troubles and can have a laxative effect.

PER SERVING: 320 Calories, 18.2 g Total Carbs, 2.4 g Fiber, 10.5 g Sugar Alcohols, 5.3 g Net Carbs, 8.4 g Protein, 28.4 g Fat

WHIPPED CREAM

Making your own whipped cream is super simple, and it's an important Keto skill to have in your back pocket! You don't need the sugar or added chemicals that the store-bought versions offer; it's just as good with the three simple ingredients below. Soon you'll be whipping up ultra-low-carb delicious toppings for all your favorite desserts. You can even get creative and add chocolate to the mix for more fun!

Yield: 2 cups (480 g), 2 tablespoons (30 g) per serving

1 cup (240 ml) heavy cream

¼ cup (30 g) powdered erythritol

1 tsp vanilla

In a large bowl, whisk the heavy cream for 3 to 5 minutes until stiff peaks form. Add the erythritol and vanilla and whisk until incorporated.

Serve immediately or store in an airtight container in the fridge for up to 3 days.

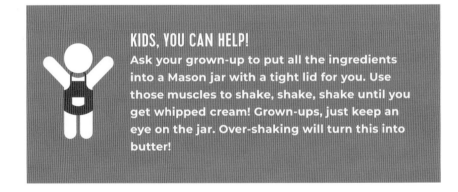

KIDS, YOU CAN HELP!
Ask your grown-up to put all the ingredients into a Mason jar with a tight lid for you. Use those muscles to shake, shake, shake until you get whipped cream! Grown-ups, just keep an eye on the jar. Over-shaking will turn this into butter!

PER SERVING: 50 Calories, 2.8 g Total Carbs, 0 g Fiber, 2.3 g Sugar Alcohols, 0.5 g Net Carbs, 0 g Protein, 5 g Fat

BREAKFAST STROMBOLI

Weekends are a great time to slow down a bit. This recipe takes a little extra time but is definitely worth the effort. The dough is mozzarella based and might be a bit tricky at first, but it's worth the delicious golden crust it forms around your scrambled eggs and bacon.

Serves: 6

4 slices bacon

5 large eggs, divided

2 tbsp (28 g) butter

1½ cups (170 g) shredded mozzarella cheese

¾ cup (84 g) blanched, finely ground almond flour

2 oz (56 g) cream cheese

½ tsp baking soda

Preheat the oven to 375°F (190°C) and line a large baking sheet with parchment.

Fry the bacon in a skillet over medium heat until it's crispy and fully cooked, about 10 to 15 minutes. Set aside to cool.

In a large bowl, whisk four of the eggs and add any preferred seasoning.

In a skillet over medium heat, melt the butter. Pour the eggs into the pan and stir occasionally for 5 to 7 minutes, until the eggs are scrambled and fluffy. Set aside.

In a large microwave-safe bowl, toss the mozzarella and almond flour together. Break the cream cheese into small pieces in the bowl and microwave for 1 minute.

Stir the mixture until a soft ball of dough forms. Sprinkle the baking soda over the dough and stir in the remaining egg. If the dough becomes too cold to work with, microwave it in 15-second intervals.

Wet your hands and press the dough out onto the parchment into a rectangle about 6 inches (15 cm) long and 4 inches (10 cm) wide. Place the long side of the rectangle closest to you. Spoon the scrambled eggs into the center of the rectangle, leaving about 1 inch (2.5 cm) of dough empty on each side.

Crumble the bacon and sprinkle it over the eggs. Fold the sides of the dough toward the center, covering the eggs and bacon. Seal the top of the dough together by pinching or folding over if needed.

Bake for 20 to 25 minutes or until golden. Let the stromboli cool for at least 10 minutes before slicing.

Slice into 6 (1-inch [2.5-cm]) pieces to serve.

PER SERVING: 313 Calories, 6.3 g Total Carbs, 1.5 g Fiber, 4.8 g Net Carbs, 18.8 g Protein, 23.1g Fat

BACON-WRAPPED EGG CUPS

I've been making egg cups for years but only recently thought to wrap them in bacon. This is a great perk of a Ketogenic lifestyle; bacon isn't off-limits! The fat and protein are important to helping you hit your daily nutrient goals. The eggs cooking at the same time as the bacon gives these egg cups a really salty and savory taste throughout every bite. The kiddos may enjoy these with just a bit of cheese, but, grown-ups, feel free to use your favorite add-ins! Chopped onions, green bell peppers, ham or even spinach make great additions!

Yield: 6 egg cups, 1 per serving

6 large eggs

¼ cup (60 ml) heavy whipping cream

¼ tsp ground black pepper

6 slices bacon

¾ cup (84 g) shredded sharp cheddar cheese

Preheat the oven to 375°F (190°C) and spray a muffin tin with nonstick spray.

In a large bowl, whisk the eggs, whipping cream and pepper and set aside. Line each muffin tin with a slice of bacon around the edges.

Evenly pour the egg mixture into the center of each tin and sprinkle with 2 tablespoons (7 g) of cheddar.

Bake for 25 minutes or until the bacon is cooked and the egg is firm.

Serve warm.

PER SERVING: 212 Calories, 1.2 g Total Carbs, 0 g Fiber, 1.2 g Net Carbs, 12.7 g Protein, 16.6 g Fat

CRUNCHY GRANOLA POWER BOWL

Smoothie bowls are tasty and also lots of fun! This recipe uses sour cream to give your smoothie bowl some tang in place of sugar-loaded yogurt. Let the kids get creative and decorate their own bowl with fun toppings! Shredded unsweetened coconut, low-carb chocolate chips, fruit slices and nuts are all healthy options that will give them energy for the day ahead.

Serves: 4

Granola

¼ cup (62 g) chopped pecans

¼ cup (55 g) chopped almonds

2 tbsp (28 g) unsalted, shelled sunflower seeds

1 tbsp (6 g) golden ground flax

2 tbsp (30 ml) water

2 tbsp (25 g) granular erythritol

1 tsp vanilla extract

¼ tsp cinnamon

Smoothie

12 frozen strawberries

12 frozen blackberries

2 tbsp (30 g) sour cream

2 tbsp (30 ml) heavy whipping cream

2 tbsp (15 g) powdered erythritol

Preheat the oven to 350°F (180°C). Line a large baking sheet with parchment.

Make the granola. In a large bowl, mix together the pecans, almonds, sunflower seeds, flax, water, granular erythritol, vanilla and cinnamon. Spread the mixture onto the baking sheet. Bake for 15 minutes, stirring after 7 minutes. Allow to cool completely.

Make the smoothie. In a blender, blend the strawberries, blackberries, sour cream, heavy whipping cream and powdered erythritol until the mixture is thick but spoonable, about 1 minute.

To assemble, spoon the smoothie evenly into four bowls. Top with granola and serve immediately.

PER SERVING (GRANOLA): 128 Calories, 8.6 g Total Carbs, 2.5 g Fiber, 4.5 g Sugar Alcohols, 1.6 g Net Carbs, 3.2 g Protein, 11 g Fat

PER SERVING (SMOOTHIE): 64 Calories, 11.4 g Total Carbs, 2.6 g Fiber, 4.5 g Sugar Alcohols, 4.25 g Net Carbs, 0.9 g Protein, 3.9 g Fat

BERRYLICIOUS BREAKFAST POPS

Hot summer days call for smoothie pops! Sometimes kids don't like to stop and sit down for breakfast immediately after they wake up. This recipe skips excessive amounts of sugar, making it acceptable for any time of the day! Make sure to read the labels for your frozen fruit and consider chopping and freezing fresh fruit yourself. Even though some packages say there's no added sugar, the amount of carbs in a serving is higher than if you were to prepare and freeze them at home yourself.

Yield: 6 berry pops, 1 per serving

4 oz (112 g) cream cheese

¼ cup (60 ml) heavy whipping cream

¼ cup (30 g) powdered erythritol

1 cup (160 g) chopped, frozen strawberries

½ cup (75 g) frozen blackberries

2 tbsp (30 g) sour cream

1 tbsp (14 g) coconut oil

Place the cream cheese, whipping cream, erythritol, strawberries, blackberries, sour cream and coconut oil into a blender and blend until smooth. Pour into six standard-size molds and place in the freezer for at least 2 hours.

To remove the pops from the molds, dip the mold into warm water for 30 seconds. Serve frozen.

PER SERVING: 139 Calories, 10.9 g Total Carbs, 1.2 g Fiber, 6 g Sugar Alcohols, 3.68 g Net Carbs, 1.5 g Protein, 13.3 g Fat

THE FLUFFIEST COCONUT FLOUR PANCAKES

When it comes to pancakes, it's always the fluffier the better. These pillowy coconut flour pancakes are so good that when you sink your teeth into them first thing in the morning, you'll think you're still dreaming! Even better, with coconut flour, we avoid any nut sensitivities to create a breakfast for everyone! Top them with a dollop of sugar-free Whipped Cream (page 124) to add a little more WOW to the meal!

Yield: 6 pancakes, 1 per serving

⅓ cup (35 g) coconut flour

2 tbsp (25 g) granular erythritol

½ tsp baking soda

2 eggs

½ tsp vanilla extract

4 tbsp (56 g) butter, divided

⅓ cup (80 ml) unsweetened almond milk

2 tbsp (30 ml) water

Low-carb syrup or sugar-free Whipped Cream (page 124), for serving

In a large bowl, mix together the coconut flour, erythritol and baking soda. Add the eggs, vanilla, 2 tablespoons (28 g) of the butter, almond milk and water. Mix until a thick but pourable batter forms.

In a skillet over medium heat, melt the remaining 2 tablespoons (28 g) of butter. Add 2 tablespoons (30 ml) of batter to the pan for each pancake, working in batches as needed. Cook for 2 to 4 minutes per side, until the edges begin to puff, then flip and cook for 1 to 3 minutes.

Serve warm with low-carb syrup or sugar-free Whipped Cream.

PER SERVING: 89 Calories, 6.8 g Total Carbs, 2.2 g Fiber, 3 g Sugar Alcohols, 1.7 g Net Carbs, 2.9 g Protein, 6.4 g Fat

MAKE-AHEAD BREAKFAST SANDWICH

You can make this tasty breakfast ahead of time AND grab it and go in the morning . . .
It doesn't get any better than that! Older kids will love taking charge of their own meal
and grabbing one of these out of the freezer and warming it up on their way out the door
for the day. The homemade sausage will taste so much better than store-bought, because
it doesn't have any fillers or preservatives. Even better, you can add more of your favorite
herbs if you desire so it's exactly the flavor your family loves. This imaginative sandwich
breaks all the rules, using savory sausage patties as buns, which cuts the carbs and gives
you a healthy dose of protein to help power you through your whole day.

Yield: 6 sandwiches

2 lb (908 g) ground pork

1 tbsp (5 g) fresh chopped sage

1 tsp garlic powder

1 tsp ground thyme

1 tsp ground fennel

1 tsp paprika

½ tsp ground black pepper

3 tbsp (42 g) butter

6 large eggs

¼ cup (60 ml) heavy whipping cream

8 slices cheddar

FREEZE IT!
**Place plastic-wrapped
sandwiches into a large
gallon-size sealed
freezer bag. To reheat,
remove the plastic wrap,
running under warm
water if needed. Reheat
in the microwave for
1½ minutes or until it's
fully thawed and hot.**

In a large bowl, mix the ground pork with the sage, garlic powder,
thyme, fennel, paprika and pepper. Separate the sausage into twelve
round patties, about ¼ inch (6 mm) thick.

Fry the patties in a skillet over medium heat until they are completely
cooked through and no pink remains, about 5 to 7 minutes. Set aside.

Drain the grease from the pan and place it back on the stove. Melt
the butter in the skillet over medium heat.

In a large bowl, whisk the eggs with the cream and pour it into
the skillet.

Cover the eggs and let them cook until they are mostly firm, but a
little liquid remains, about 5 to 7 minutes, and then flip. It will look
like a giant omelet. Turn off the heat and let the eggs finish cooking
for 1 to 3 minutes, until no liquid remains.

Remove the eggs from the pan and place them onto a cutting board.
Cut the eggs into six pieces or use a glass to cut six rounds from the
eggs, if preferred.

To build your sandwiches, place one egg piece onto one sausage
patty. Top with cheese and place a second sausage patty on top of
the cheese.

Enjoy immediately or wrap each sandwich tightly in plastic wrap and
store in the fridge for up to 5 days.

PER SERVING: 642 Calories, 2 g Total Carbs, 0.5 g Fiber, 1.5 g Net Carbs,
38.6 g Protein, 51.6 g Fat

SAUSAGE AND EGG BAKE

If you're anything like me, it doesn't matter how early you get up; the time always seems to get away from you in the mornings. While it's true that preparing healthy meals takes longer than prepackaged food, there's a lot you can do to minimize your daily cooking with a little meal prep. This is a favorite of mine to make because the kids love it, and it cooks up easily on a lazy Sunday afternoon, which means there's plenty of breakfast for the entire week with minimal effort.

Serves: 8

1 lb (454 g) pork ground breakfast sausage

2 tbsp (28 g) butter

½ cup (120 ml) heavy whipping cream

¼ tsp ground black pepper

2 oz (56 g) softened cream cheese

¼ tsp xanthan gum, for thickening

8 large eggs

1 cup (112 g) shredded mild cheddar cheese, divided

Preheat the oven to 400°F (200°C) and prepare a 9 x 9-inch (20 x 20-cm) baking dish with nonstick spray. Set aside.

In a skillet over medium heat, brown the breakfast sausage until no pink remains, about 7 to 10 minutes. When fully cooked, add the butter to the pan. Do not drain the sausage grease first; this will help make the sauce.

Pour in the heavy cream and add the pepper and cream cheese. Stir until the cream cheese is melted and smooth, about 45 seconds. Sprinkle in the xanthan gum and gently stir. Bring the mixture to a boil for 45 seconds then reduce the heat to simmer for 5 minutes to thicken.

In a large pan over medium heat, crack the eggs and cook for 5 to 7 minutes, stirring frequently until fluffy and scrambled.

Pour half of the sausage gravy in the bottom of the baking dish. Place half of the scrambled eggs on top of the gravy and top with ½ cup (56 g) of cheddar. Repeat the sausage gravy and egg layers and top the casserole with the remaining ½ cup (56 g) cheese.

Bake for 15 to 17 minutes or until the casserole is bubbling and the cheese begins to brown on top.

Let the casserole cool for 10 minutes, then slice and serve.

PER SERVING: 387 Calories, 3.8 g Total Carbs, 0.4 g Fiber, 3.4 g Net Carbs, 18.6 g Protein, 32.7 g Fat

FAUXGURT

Yogurt is creamy, delicious and perfect for everything from smoothies to parfaits. But most yogurts are loaded with sugar—up to 30 grams per serving in some of the more popular brands. You might find some lower-carb options on the grocery store shelves, but it's pretty tough to find one that also has high fat. This recipe is your solution and your new favorite breakfast!

Yield: 1 cup (120 g), ¼ cup (30 g) per serving

1 cup (240 g) sour cream

1 tbsp (15 ml) heavy whipping cream

2 tbsp (15 g) powdered erythritol

½ tsp vanilla extract

Your choice of mix-ins, such as nuts, strawberries and blueberries or granola

In a large bowl, mix the sour cream, heavy cream, erythritol and vanilla. Serve with your choice of nuts, berries or granola from the Crunchy Granola Power Bowl (page 131).

Store covered in fridge for up to 5 days.

CUSTOMIZE IT!
Swap out the vanilla for another favorite extract or fresh, pureed low-carb berries!

PER SERVING: 125 Calories, 6.4 g Total Carbs, 0 g Fiber, 4.5 g Sugar Alcohols, 1.9 g Net Carbs, 1.3 g Protein, 12.6 g Fat

SWEET TREATS YOU'LL LOVE

SWEET TREATS ARE EXTRA SPECIAL. They help us express our creativity, bond with our families and celebrate some of life's most important moments. Because cooking yummy desserts is often one of the first cooking adventures little ones have in the kitchen, these recipes are easy to follow so you can truly enjoy the time spent together.

These treats will impress the whole family and even surprise those who aren't familiar with the Ketogenic diet. Your friends will be amazed that something so delicious can also be good for you! Each recipe in this chapter serves as a great opportunity to talk to your kiddos about how putting nutritious food into your body doesn't mean you ever have to miss out.

From Confetti Vanilla Birthday Cake (page 146) to celebrate another trip around the sun, to Double-Chocolate Brownies (page 152) for all of your chocolate lovers, this chapter is packed with a variety of delectable desserts to keep everyone smiling.

EASY PEASY LEMON LOAF

This lemon loaf is a deliciously tangy and sweet pound cake–style loaf. My kids adore lemons and cake, of course, so this dish is the perfect excuse to enjoy both for dessert— or even breakfast! I love this recipe for kids because it's also very easy to make together. The ingredients are things you may already have lying around the house, which makes it perfect for a last-minute kitchen adventure. If you're a fan of poppy seeds, feel free to add a sprinkle to the batter before cooking!

Serves: 12

2 tbsp (28 g) butter, for greasing the pan

2 cups (224 g) blanched, finely ground almond flour

¾ cup (150 g) granular erythritol

1 tbsp (12 g) baking powder

4 eggs

½ cup (120 g) sour cream

1 tsp vanilla extract

2 oz (56 g) softened cream cheese

½ cup (120 ml) melted butter

1 tbsp (10 g) lemon zest

2 tbsp (30 ml) lemon juice

Preheat the oven to 350°F (180°C). Generously butter a 9 x 5–inch (23 x 13–cm) loaf pan and set aside.

In a large bowl, whisk togehter the almond flour, erythritol and baking powder.

Crack the eggs into the bowl. Add the sour cream, vanilla and cream cheese to the bowl and stir until a thick batter begins to form.

Pour in the melted butter and continue stirring until the ingredients are fully mixed. Add the lemon zest and juice to the batter. Stir until the batter is mostly smooth.

Pour the batter into the loaf pan, scraping down the sides of the bowl as needed. Place the pan into the oven and bake for 50 minutes. The top of the loaf will turn dark golden brown and a toothpick will come out clean when it's completely cooked. Add 5 to 10 minutes of baking time if needed.

Let the loaf cool completely before slicing; otherwise, the slices will fall apart. Allow at least 2 hours for best results.

PER SERVING: 245 Calories, 19 g Total Carbs, 2 g Fiber, 12 g Sugar Alcohols, 5 g Net Carbs, 7.2 g Protein, 21 g Fat

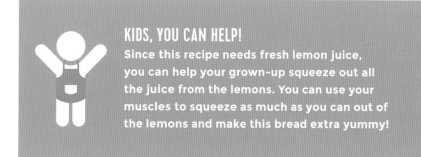

KIDS, YOU CAN HELP!
Since this recipe needs fresh lemon juice, you can help your grown-up squeeze out all the juice from the lemons. You can use your muscles to squeeze as much as you can out of the lemons and make this bread extra yummy!

CONFETTI VANILLA BIRTHDAY CAKE

This recipe is one of my personal favorites, and it took a lot of trial and error to get it just right. Birthdays are such a special time, and no one should have to feel left out because they're choosing a healthier lifestyle. This cake is slightly sweet but also has a defined butter-and-vanilla taste. The texture is similar to a classic pound cake, and the 6-inch (15-cm) pan means the cake is a bit taller and narrower than a traditional cake. Feel free to add your favorite low-carb frosting (Easy Frosting, page 149) or sugar-free Whipped Cream (page 124).

Serves: 12

½ cup (112 g) butter

4 oz (112 g) cream cheese

2 cups (224 g) blanched, finely ground almond flour

2 tsp (10 g) baking powder

1 cup (200 g) granular erythritol

1 tsp vanilla extract

½ cup (120 g) sour cream

4 large eggs

¼ cup (20 g) unsweetened shredded coconut, divided

Natural food coloring, for confetti

Easy Frosting (page 149) or Whipped Cream (page 124), for serving

Preheat the oven to 350°F (180°C). Prepare two 6-inch (15-cm) baking pans with nonstick spray.

Cut the butter and cream cheese into small chunks and place into a small microwave-safe bowl. Microwave for 30 seconds and stir. Set aside.

In a large bowl, mix the almond flour, baking powder and granular erythritol. Slowly pour the melted butter mixture into the large bowl and mix.

Add the vanilla and sour cream to the bowl. Stir in the eggs until just combined. The batter will be pourable.

Among three small bowls, separate the shredded coconut. Place 1 to 3 drops of food coloring in each bowl and stir with a toothpick. Let it dry for 5 minutes, and then mix into a single bowl. Sprinkle the coconut over the cake batter and gently fold in.

Pour the batter evenly into the prepared baking pans. Place the pans into the oven and bake for 20 to 25 minutes or until golden and mostly firm. A toothpick should come out mostly clean.

Let the cakes cool completely, for at least 2 hours, before removing them from the pans. They firm up as they cool, and moving too soon can cause them to fall apart.

Place the bottom cake on a cake stand and add a layer of frosting to the top of it, as evenly as possible. Carefully place the second cake on top and spread a layer of frosting on the very top. Slice and serve at room temperature with low-carb Easy Frosting (page 149) or Whipped Cream (page 124).

Store covered in the fridge for up to 4 days for maximum freshness.

PER SERVING: 255 Calories, 23.6 g Total Carbs, 2.2 g Fiber, 16 g Sugar Alcohols, 5.4 g Net Carbs, 7.5 g Protein, 21.9 g Fat

EASY FROSTING

Let's be real . . . the best part of any cake is its frosting! Luckily, this recipe is very easy to master and customize to your favorite flavor profile. The key to perfect frosting is to make sure that the butter is just softened, but not melted. If it's too melted, then your frosting will be runny and won't stay on the cake or cupcakes as well. If it gets too warm in your kitchen and turns runny, just pop it into the freezer for a few minutes to let it firm up—just be sure you remember to take it out!

Yield: 2 cups (240 g), 2 tablespoons (15 g) per serving

8 oz (226 g) softened cream cheese

½ cup (112 g) softened butter

½ cup (60 g) powdered erythritol

1 tsp vanilla extract

In a large bowl, whip the cream cheese, butter, erythritol and vanilla together until fluffy, about 3 to 5 minutes.

Use immediately or store in airtight container for up to 1 week.

FOR CHOCOLATE FROSTING:
Add 2 extra tablespoons (15 g) of powdered erythritol plus 4 tablespoons (20 g) of cocoa powder.

FOR PEANUT BUTTER FROSTING:
Add 4 tablespoons (60 g) peanut powder.

PER SERVING: 99 Calories, 5.1 g Total Carbs, 0 g Fiber, 4.5 g Sugar Alcohols, 0.6 g Net Carbs, 0.9 g Protein, 10.5 g Fat

CHOCOLATE CHIP COOKIES

These are the ultimate gooey and chewy cookies! With this healthier spin on a traditional recipe, you can relax and enjoy a treat with the family and know that you're all making a healthier choice. Besides being lower in carbs, you're also getting a nice protein boost from the nut flour!

Yield: 10 cookies, 1 per serving

2 tbsp (30 ml) melted butter

½ cup (100 g) granular erythritol

2 tbsp (32 g) no-sugar-added natural peanut butter

1 large egg

1 tsp vanilla extract

1 cup (112 g) blanched, finely ground almond flour

½ tsp baking powder

¼ tsp salt

¼ cup (45 g) low-carb chocolate chips

PER SERVING: 178 Calories, 9.1 g Total Carbs, 3.1g Fiber, 16 g Sugar Alcohols, 6 g Net Carbs, 6 g Protein, 14 g Fat

Preheat the oven to 350°F (180°C) and line a large baking sheet with parchment.

In a large bowl, mix together the butter, erythritol and peanut butter until mostly smooth. Add the egg and vanilla to the mixture and stir.

In a medium bowl, mix the almond flour, baking powder and salt. Add this dry mixture to the large bowl slowly, stirring until a dough forms. Add the chocolate chips.

Roll the mixture into ten balls and place onto the baking sheet, leaving 2 inches (5 cm) of space between them. Bake for 15 minutes or until the edges begin to brown. Allow the cookies to cool for at least 20 minutes before eating.

STICKY DOUGH
You may find that a lot of Keto doughs are much stickier than you're used to working with in traditional baking. This is because the almond flour and the lack of gluten affect the dough's form. Sticky dough doesn't mean you're doing it wrong though. Wetting your hands with water then shaking them gently will make handling the dough much easier.

KIDS, YOU CAN HELP!
This is a great recipe to practice measuring! Help your grown-up by measuring out the ingredients and pouring them carefully into the bowl.

DOUBLE-CHOCOLATE BROWNIES

It took me a couple years to find the perfect Keto brownie recipe, but lots of trial, error and messy aprons led me to these decadent and fudgy beauties! You might need an ice-cold glass of unsweetened almond milk to wash these down because they are RICH! But they're everything a brownie should be, made even better by the extra-special secret ingredient—dark cocoa powder! Make sure you don't skip the salt because it will give the brownies the perfect balance to the sweetness.

Serves: 12

½ cup (112 g) butter

1 cup (120 g) powdered erythritol

2 eggs

2 tsp (10 ml) vanilla extract

¾ cup (84 g) blanched, finely ground almond flour

¼ cup (20 g) unsweetened dark cocoa powder

1 tsp baking powder

⅛ tsp salt

¼ cup (45 g) low-carb chocolate chips

Preheat the oven to 350°F (180°C) and line an 8 x 8–inch (20 x 20-cm) baking dish with parchment. Set aside.

In a large bowl, cream the butter and erythritol. Mix in the eggs and vanilla.

Add the almond flour, cocoa powder, baking powder and salt and stir. The mixture will be thick.

Fold in the chocolate chips and scrape the batter into the baking dish.

Bake for 25 to 30 minutes. A toothpick will come out clean. It may appear a little jiggly, but almond flour sets and firms as it cools. Let the brownies cool for at least 30 minutes. Slice into twelve pieces to serve.

CUSTOMIZE IT!
Feel free to add your favorite mix-ins. Chopped pecans, extra chocolate chips or even topping these brownies with chocolate Easy Frosting (page 149) are great ways to take them to the next level!

PER SERVING: 129 Calories, 16.9 g Total Carbs, 1.8 g Fiber, 12.5 g Sugar Alcohols, 2.65 g Net Carbs, 3.3 g Protein, 11.5 g Fat

MINI CHOCOLATE CUPCAKES

Chocolate cake has forever been my favorite, and these sweet mini cupcakes capture those flavors in a treat that's perfectly sized for your little ones' hands. Plus, they'll have a blast decorating them! These are not only moist and fluffy but also easy to make, and they contain ingredients you might already have in the pantry. The chocolate is flavorful but not so rich that it would overwhelm a little one's palate. The mayo in the cake gives it extra moisture, but feel free to swap for equal amounts sour cream or even plain unsweetened Greek yogurt. To make these even more delectable, top them with a small scoop of Easy Frosting (page 149)!

Yield: 24 mini cupcakes, 2 per serving

1 cup (112 g) blanched, finely ground almond flour

½ cup (100 g) granular erythritol

¼ cup (20 g) cocoa powder

¼ cup (56 g) softened butter

1 tsp vanilla extract

1 tbsp (13 g) mayo

2 eggs

⅓ cup (80 ml) unsweetened vanilla almond milk

Easy Frosting (page 149), for serving

Preheat the oven to 350°F (175°C). Prepare a 24-well mini muffin tin with liners.

In a large bowl, mix the almond flour, erythritol and cocoa powder until fully combined. Mix in the butter, vanilla and mayo. Crack the eggs into the bowl and stir until completely combined, and then stir in the almond milk.

Place a heaping tablespoon (10 g) of batter into each well. Place the tin in the oven for 12 to 15 minutes or until a toothpick comes out clean. Allow the cupcakes to cool for at least 20 minutes before serving.

Top with Easy Frosting or enjoy by themselves. Store in an airtight container in the fridge for up to 4 days for maximum freshness.

PER SERVING: 109 Calories, 12.2 g Total Carbs, 1.36 g Fiber, 8 g Sugar Alcohols, 2.81 g Net Carbs, 3.7 g Protein, 8.9 g Fat

STRAWBERRY-LEMONADE FLUFF

This sweet and sour fluff is just the thing to capture a little extra sunshine in your day. This spoonable dessert whips up in no time and is bursting with that sour flavor all the little ones seem to love. Eat it out of the bowl or even freeze it into popsicle molds for a delicious high-fat treat that keeps the little tummies full and happy.

Yield: 2 cups (490 g), ¼ cup (61 g) per serving

8 oz (226 g) softened cream cheese

¼ cup (30 g) powdered erythritol

¼ cup (60 ml) heavy whipping cream

2 tbsp (28 g) coconut oil

Zest and juice from ½ lemon

6 strawberries

In a large bowl, whip the cream cheese, erythritol and heavy whipping cream until smooth.

Add the coconut oil and continue whipping until fluffy. Add the lemon zest and juice to the bowl.

Slice the tops off of the strawberries and place them into a large bowl. With a fork, mash until mostly soft but a few chunks remain.

Fold the mashed strawberries into the cream cheese fluff.

Cover and place into the fridge to firm up for at least 2 hours. Serve cold.

PER SERVING: 155 Calories, 6.9 g Total Carbs, 0.3 g Fiber, 4.5 g Sugar Alcohols, 2.1 g Net Carbs, 1.9 g Protein, 16.1 g Fat

MINT CHOCOLATE CHIP POPS

Keto ice cream is super easy to make, and these pops simplify the process even more! The fluffy heavy cream makes these super light tasting with just a hint of sweetness to satisfy that craving for ice cream. Making them into individual servings helps keep portions under control without thinking about it, not to mention they're more on the go—just like your lifestyle. These popsicles won't be green like you might expect to see because there are no added dyes, but if that's a must for your little ones, you can find a natural food coloring and add a few drops of green.

Serves: 8

1 cup (240 ml) heavy whipping cream

½ cup (120 ml) almond milk

½ cup (60 g) powdered erythritol

1 tsp vanilla extract

½ tsp mint extract

¼ cup (45 g) low-carb chocolate chips

In a large bowl, whisk the heavy cream, almond milk, erythritol, vanilla and mint until soft peaks form, for 3 to 5 minutes. Fold in the chocolate chips.

Pour into eight 4-inch (10-cm) popsicle molds.

Freeze for at least 4 hours. Serve cold.

PER SERVING: 115 Calories, 12.4 g Total Carbs, 1 g Fiber, 9.8 g Sugar Alcohols, 1.6 g Net Carbs, 0.3 g Protein, 11.3 g Fat

MUG CAKE

A quick dessert at the end of a long day is sometimes just what you need! This recipe takes just 6 minutes from start to finish and is perfect for sharing. It's not overly sweet and has the texture of a moist sponge cake. Feel free to add a few chocolate chips or chopped nuts to the batter before cooking. This is a dish so simple that the older kids can even make it on their own!

Serves: 2

1 tbsp (14 g) butter

3 tbsp (23 g) powdered erythritol

1 egg

½ tsp vanilla extract

3 tbsp (21 g) blanched, finely ground almond flour

½ tsp baking powder

1½ tbsp (7 g) unsweetened dark cocoa powder

Place the butter in a 12-ounce (355-ml) mug and microwave for 15 seconds to melt. Add the erythritol and stir until a paste forms. Add the egg and stir.

Pour in the vanilla and stir again. Add the almond flour, baking powder and cocoa powder and mix until fully combined and a wet batter forms.

Place the mug into the microwave for 1 minute. Serve warm.

TOPPING IDEAS
This mug cake can be eaten alone but also tastes great with light and airy sugar-free Whipped Cream (page 124)! You can also add a drizzle of your favorite nut butter or add sliced berries to add a fresh-tasting twist!

PER SERVING: 153 Calories, 19.7 g Total Carbs, 1.9 g Fiber, 13.5 g Sugar Alcohols, 4.4 g Net Carbs, 6.4 g Protein, 12 g Fat

EASY NO-CHURN VANILLA ICE CREAM

If you're looking for low-carb, Keto-friendly ice cream at the supermarket, you may be surprised that there aren't many options. There are a few companies that offer them, but many of them are marketed as protein ice creams and often have very low fat content. Luckily, it's super easy to make your own at home! The kids will love getting to choose the flavors they want, taste testing and helping to whip the cream. For even more fun, add a serving of Crackling Chocolate Shell (page 182) to the top of your bowl of ice cream! The kids will love watching it freeze before their eyes and enjoy cracking it open with their spoons to enjoy the delicious chocolate pieces.

Yield: 3 cups (720 ml), ½ cup (120 ml) per serving

1 cup (240 ml) heavy whipping cream

3 tbsp (23 g) powdered erythritol

2 tsp (10 ml) vanilla extract

¼ cup (60 ml) unsweetened vanilla almond milk

In a large, deep bowl, add the whipping cream, erythritol, vanilla and almond milk. Use a whisk to beat the mixture until fluffy. Pour it into a loaf pan, cover and freeze for at least 3 hours. Let it sit for 5 to 10 minutes to soften before scooping.

FOR STRAWBERRY ICE CREAM:
In a large bowl, mash six ripe strawberries (with tops removed). Fold into the vanilla ice cream.

FOR CHOCOLATE ICE CREAM:
Whisk in 2 tablespoons (10 g) of cocoa powder and one additional tablespoon (18 g) of powdered erythritol to the heavy cream mixture before freezing.

MAKE IT YOUR OWN!
Feel free to add your favorite low-carb toppings, such as chopped pecans, berries or even a drizzle of Crackling Chocolate Shell (page 182)!

PER SERVING: 224 Calories, 4.6 g Total Carbs, 1.5 g Fiber, 4.5 g Sugar Alcohols, 3.2 g Net Carbs, 29.3 g Protein, 9.3 g Fat

STEP-UP-YOUR-GAME SAUCES

SAUCES NOT ONLY ENHANCE THE FLAVOR OF A DISH, they also help us hide the tastes we less than love. This is especially true for kiddos. In either case, the low-carb sauces in this chapter are perfect for dipping, topping and even slathering your food with.

Many store-bought sauces are either loaded up with sugar to help the taste or boosted with other unnecessary ingredients to help hold the product together and keep it shelf stable. With these fresh and easy sauces, from the savory Mouthwatering Marinara (page 170) to the sweet Crackling Chocolate Shell (page 182), you'll know exactly what you're putting in your body, and you'll be more than happy to put it on your food!

CLASSIC KETCHUP

Ketchup is a kid favorite and goes with so many things, from chicken nuggets to burgers and low-carb veggie fries. This sauce doesn't have to be left out on a low-carb diet. Regular ketchup has ingredients such as high fructose corn syrup, which are best avoided on a Ketogenic diet. This recipe uses erythritol, but you can always swap for your favorite low-carb sweetener, such as Stevia, or omit the sweetener all together if the tomatoes are sweet enough for you.

Yield: ¾ cup (180 ml), 1 tablespoon (15 ml) per serving

1 cup (245 g) tomato sauce

1 tsp white vinegar

½ tsp onion powder

¼ tsp garlic powder

⅛ tsp ground cloves

2 tsp (8 g) granular erythritol

2 tsp (10 g) butter

Place the tomato sauce, vinegar, onion powder, garlic powder, cloves, erythritol and butter into a saucepan over medium heat. Bring to a boil and then reduce to a low simmer for 30 minutes, stirring and scraping down the sides as necessary.

Chill in the fridge before serving. Store in an airtight jar in the refrigerator for up to 1 week. You can also use this recipe as a base for the BBQ Sauce (page 169).

PER SERVING: 25 Calories, 2.9 g Total Carbs, 0.4 g Fiber, 0.8 g Sugar Alcohols, 1.7 g Net Carbs, 0.3 g Protein, 1.8 g Fat

BBQ SAUCE

The uses for BBQ sauce are pretty much endless. My kids especially love to dip their chicken nuggets in it! Using the Classic Ketchup (page 166) as a base, we can make a delicious rich and tangy sauce that's perfect for anything from the Zesty BBQ Drumsticks (page 62) to your own smoky creation!

Yield: ½ cup (120 ml), 1 tablespoon (15 ml) per serving

½ cup (120 ml) Classic Ketchup (page 166)

1 tbsp (13 g) granular erythritol

2 tbsp (30 ml) Worcestershire sauce

¼ tsp liquid smoke

In a small saucepan, mix the ketchup, erythritol, Worcestershire and liquid smoke and simmer for 5 minutes.

Remove from the heat and use immediately or store in an airtight jar in the refrigerator for up to 1 week.

PER SERVING: 29 Calories, 4.9 g Total Carbs, 0.4 g Fiber, 1.9 g Sugar Alcohols, 2.6 g Net Carbs, 0.4 g Protein, 1.8 g Fat

MOUTHWATERING MARINARA

Marinara is hands-down my favorite savory sauce. You can use it for dipping chicken, topping pizza and so much more! Most store-bought marinara is filled with sugar to enhance the taste, but we definitely don't need it. This recipe brings out the natural flavors of the tomatoes to give you a perfectly pleasing sauce with zero added sugar. Canned tomatoes often have an acidic taste, which the sugar in sauces tends to neutralize. Butter also works great to neutralize that acidity and adds an extra boost of fat without any extra sugar!

Yield: 2 cups (480 ml), ¼ cup (60 ml) per serving

4 tbsp (56 g) butter, divided

¼ cup (40 g) chopped onion

½ tsp minced garlic

1 (6-oz [170-g]) can tomato paste

2 cups (480 ml) chicken broth

½ tsp dried basil

¼ tsp oregano

In a saucepan over medium heat, melt 2 tablespoons (28 g) of the butter. Add the onion and sauté for 2 to 3 minutes until the onion becomes soft and fragrant. Add the minced garlic and sauté for 30 seconds.

Add the tomato paste, broth, basil and oregano. Stir until the tomato paste and broth have fully combined. Bring it to a boil, and then reduce and let the sauce simmer for 10 to 15 minutes, stirring occasionally until the sauce begins to thicken. Add the remaining butter, stir until melted and then remove from the heat to cool.

Store in an airtight jar and refrigerate for up to 4 days.

PER SERVING: 74 Calories, 5.4 g Total Carbs, 1.4 g Fiber, 3.9 g Net Carbs, 1 g Protein, 44.3 g Fat

CHEESE SAUCE

This is my go-to cheese sauce. It's versatile and so simple! You can make it as a base for any casserole you want to whip up, or pour it over steamed veggies, such as broccoli. Switching out the type of cheese can totally change the flavor profile. Cheddar cheese sauce tastes great with chicken, but if you want a bit of a kick, try using shredded pepper Jack and pour it over some thinly sliced steak with peppers and onions for a cheesesteak bowl. The possibilities are endless!

Yield: 1½ cups (360 ml), 2 tablespoons (30 ml) per serving

2 tbsp (28 g) butter

½ cup (120 ml) heavy whipping cream

1 oz (28 g) softened cream cheese

⅛ tsp ground black pepper

1 cup (112 g) freshly shredded sharp cheddar cheese

In a saucepan over medium heat, melt the butter. Pour in the heavy cream and whisk in the cream cheese until smooth, for 2 to 3 minutes.

Once the sauce is smooth, sprinkle with pepper and turn off the heat. Add the shredded cheese and whisk quickly until all the cheese is melted. The sauce may seem thicker and elastic; this is normal. When you bake it or use it over veggies, the steam will help make it extra creamy and loosen it up.

PER SERVING: 115 Calories, 0.6 g Total Carbs, 0 g Fiber, 0.6 g Net Carbs, 2.9 g Protein, 10.9 g Fat

ROCKIN' RANCH DIP

Store-bought dry ranch mixes are convenient but often contain preservatives and fillers that might not be the best choices for your Keto lifestyle. Maltodextrin is just one example of a common additive that may raise your blood glucose higher than sugar itself! Luckily, it's super easy to make ranch dip at home, and this recipe is even more delicious than any packet in the store. Make it a fun party platter with mini cups and veggie strips or even just an easy mid-week snack tray!

Yield: 1¼ cups (600 ml), 2 tablespoons (30 ml) per serving

½ cup (116 g) mayonnaise

¾ cup (180 g) full-fat sour cream

½ tsp garlic powder

½ tsp dried dill

½ tsp seasoned salt

Cucumber slices, celery sticks and carrots, for serving

In a large bowl, mix the mayo, sour cream, garlic powder, dill and salt until fully combined.

Cover and chill for at least 20 minutes in the fridge. Serve with cucumber slices, celery sticks and carrots or your favorite low-carb veggies.

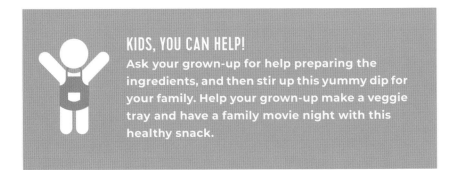

KIDS, YOU CAN HELP!
Ask your grown-up for help preparing the ingredients, and then stir up this yummy dip for your family. Help your grown-up make a veggie tray and have a family movie night with this healthy snack.

PER SERVING: 109 Calories, 0.7 g Total Carbs, 0.02 g Fiber, 0.8 g Net Carbs, 0.5 g Protein, 11.6 g Fat

TARTAR SAUCE

Tangy, creamy and just a tad sweet—who knew tartar sauce was so easy to make? This sauce is easy to whip up fresh for any night of the week, but you can also make it and store it in the fridge for up to 1 week. This sauce might not last as long as store-bought, but it comes without all the added preservatives and is made with stuff you probably already have in the fridge! I'd call that a weeknight win. This sauce will pair perfectly with the Fish Sticks (page 55)!

Yield: 1½ cups (300 g), 2 tablespoons (25 g) per serving

1 cup (240 g) mayo

½ cup (71 g) finely chopped dill pickles

2 tsp (10 ml) dill pickle juice

1 tsp fresh lemon juice

½ tsp dried minced onion

In a large bowl, mix the mayo, pickles, pickle juice, lemon juice and dried onion.

Serve immediately or place in an airtight jar in the fridge for up to 1 week.

PER SERVING: 126 Calories, 0.4 g Total Carbs, 0.1 g Fiber, 0.3 g Net Carbs, 0.2 g Protein, 13.8 g Fat

RESTAURANT-STYLE GUACAMOLE

No more paying extra for guacamole! If you've never made your own before, you're in for a treat. The creamy avocados make a great base that's brightened up with cilantro and fresh-squeezed lime juice. The kids will love getting to help with juicing the lime and adding all the ingredients to the bowl. The tomato and onion make this dish a bit chunkier than what you may be used to at the store, but it adds so much flavor you'll never leave it out again. The kids will love dipping cheese crisps or pork rinds into this for a snack! This dish is so easy, and it will also pair well with your favorite Mexican dish, such as Cheese Shell Tacos (page 28).

Serves: 6

2 large ripe avocados, pitted and peeled

Juice of 1 lime

¼ tsp garlic powder

¼ cup (64 g) finely diced red onion

1 Roma tomato, seeded and diced

2 tbsp (2 g) fresh chopped cilantro

In a large bowl, mash the avocados with a fork until mostly smooth but leaving some chunks for texture. Add the lime juice and garlic powder and gently stir.

Gently fold in the onion, tomato and cilantro. Cover and chill for at least 20 minutes for the best flavor. Serve chilled as a side with pork rinds or on top of your favorite Mexican-style dish.

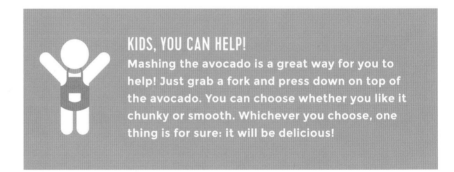

KIDS, YOU CAN HELP!
Mashing the avocado is a great way for you to help! Just grab a fork and press down on top of the avocado. You can choose whether you like it chunky or smooth. Whichever you choose, one thing is for sure: it will be delicious!

PER SERVING: 120 Calories, 8.8 g Total Carbs, 4.8 g Fiber, 4 g Net Carbs, 1.7 g Protein, 9.8 g Fat

BURGER SAUCE

If you love the tang and crunch of Big Mac sauce, then you'll love this! Many restaurants have added sugar in their "special sauce" to give it a hint of sweetness, but it's usually not needed. The ketchup has natural hints of sweetness that adding excess sugar only hides. This sauce is not only great on burgers, it makes a great dipping sauce for chicken and even veggies too!

Yield: 6 servings, 2 tablespoons (26 g) per serving

½ cup (116 g) mayo

2 tbsp (30 ml) Classic Ketchup (page 166)

2 tbsp (40 g) finely diced white onion

¼ tsp garlic powder

5 slices (35 g) dill pickle, finely diced

In a large bowl, mix the mayo, ketchup, onion, garlic powder and pickle with a rubber spatula or spoon.

Serve on top of your favorite burger, drizzle over your Everything But the Bun Cheeseburger Casserole (page 66) or use it as a dipping sauce for Jicama Fries (page 20).

Store in an airtight container or jar in the fridge for up to 1 week.

PER SERVING: 135 Calories, 1.5 g Total Carbs, 0.3 g Fiber, 0.2 g Sugar Alcohols, 1 g Net Carbs, 0.3 g Protein, 14.4 g Fat

CRACKLING CHOCOLATE SHELL

Adding a chocolate shell to my ice cream was one of my favorite parts of dessert time when I was a kid. It was always so much fun to see how fast it hardened, yet it still melted in your mouth. This very low-carb, sugar-free version does just the same, but in a much-better-for-you way. Be sure to pull this recipe out for your next make-your-own ice cream sundae bar, and pair it with the Easy No-Churn Vanilla Ice Cream (page 163)!

Serves: 4, 2 tbsp (30 ml) per serving

½ cup (120 ml) melted coconut oil

½ cup (42 g) dark cocoa powder

¼ cup (30 g) powdered erythritol

In a medium bowl, mix the coconut oil, cocoa and erythritol together.

Store in the fridge in an airtight container and warm in the microwave for 20 seconds before serving.

PER SERVING: 260 Calories, 15.8 g Total Carbs, 2 g Fiber, 9 g Sugar Alcohols, 4.8 g Net Carbs, 0 g Protein, 27 g Fat

ACKNOWLEDGMENTS

Thank you to my loves, Joey and Maya. Thank you both for inspiring me to make better choices for our family. These recipes wouldn't be here if you didn't love them. Thank you for being my taste testers and always being willing to jump into a picture to bring it to life. I appreciate your patience and encouragement. I love you both to the moon and back.

To my husband, Joe, thank you for putting up with all the trays of brownies, late work nights and listening to me ramble about food ideas constantly. You had a vision for HKM and encouraged me each day as we brought our dreams to life together. Thank you for your steadfast love and support. I love you, always and forever.

Thank you to all my friends and family for your love, kind words and ideas.

Thank you to Sarah, Caitlin and Page Street Publishing for believing in this book and making it come to life.

Thank you to all my readers for your support, kind words, feedback and excitement over my recipes—it makes all the difference.

ABOUT THE AUTHOR

SAM DILLARD, author of *The "I Love My Air Fryer" Keto Diet Recipe Book*, is the recipe creator and photographer behind Hey Keto Mama, a popular food blog that cuts carbs and strikes out sugar without sacrificing yummy flavor. Since launching in 2015, her goal has been creating quick, easy, low-carb recipes that the entire family can enjoy together. Sam's recipes have been viewed by millions and featured in numerous publications, including *Women's Health* and Shape.com. She lives in Missouri with her husband and two young children.

INDEX